I0510291

CONTEMPTIBLE

*A surgeon's battle for justice against insurance giant Cigna
and a biased federal bench*

John B Hackert, MD

Copyright © 2019 by John B Hackert, MD

All rights reserved

Cover photograph:

Atrium of the Federal Courthouse,
Eastern District of California, Sacramento Division

Second Edition

Contents

PART I

Hackert v. Cigna

Chapter 1

It's really the makings of another story but circumstances spoke and I ended up closing my practice as a colorectal surgeon and transitioned to assisting-only. If you're wondering why anyone would choose that "all guts, no glory" field, outside of Hollywood none of medicine is particularly glamorous and the grueling years of general surgery residency tend to steer the apprentice toward a subspecialty matching the temperament. Those seeking adrenaline and adventure might pursue trauma surgery. Elective intestinal procedures, in contrast, though by no means free of technical challenges are at least more predictable.

An initial step in the migration to surgical assisting was to contact the various insurance entities to discuss contracting. Would the existing agreements be continued, or tailored to the assist-only model?

In the case of Cigna the provider relations agent I reached had the somewhat distinctive name of Deedee who said in a matter of fact tone, "We don't credential assistants in your area. You'll be considered non-PAR."

To "credential" a medical provider means to formally review the physician's record, including training, licensure, board certification, hospital privileges, peer references, continuing education, regulatory sanctions, and malpractice history, usually at least every couple of years. It was no surprise that Cigna deferred credentialing for assistants. As much work as it is for a provider to fill out these endless forms, imagine the verification process on the other end.

There likewise seemed no reason to question the status of "non-PAR," an industry abbreviation for "non-participating." To me this simply meant that Cigna would pay a reasonable amount for the services rendered without the formality of maintaining a written contract. Little could I have imagined, though, just how fateful this phone call was to become.

Chapter 2

A colleague once remarked that operating comes down essentially to cutting and sewing. But unlike say a kindergarten art project, surgery tends not to be a cut-on-the-dotted-line proposition. Yet a skilled assistant can help bring the dissection plane as it's known into much better definition through techniques like "traction-countertraction": the lead surgeon places the target gently on stretch as the assistant draws the tissue oppositely, making the nearest thing to a "dotted line" appear. The surgeon then divides the membrane with a pair of scissors, for example, or a cautery device, as the assistant suctions the field and prepares for the next step. These same techniques translate to laparoscopic surgery where grasping instruments replace the hands, and the assistant might drive the camera while simultaneously retracting. In robotic procedures the assistant's role becomes even more important tableside as the primary surgeon operates from a console, unscrubbed.

The basic requirements to become a physician are four years of college focusing on biology, chemistry, physics, and calculus, followed by four years of medical school. A general surgery residency spans a minimum of five years, commonly with a separate research year. Additional subspecialty training may be acquired through a fellowship. Roughly a decade and a half of rigorous study and labor, not to mention sleep deprivation. A surgeon-as-assistant is often further seasoned by years of experience in the gown and gloves. I believe most physicians view the practice of medicine as a calling, but also feel they should be fairly paid for their knowledge and skill. Those in the profession must also shoulder the ever present threat of malpractice allegations and the hefty expense of insurance against which.

Soon after the move to assisting-only I was discouraged to receive from Cigna what seemed a modest $66.41 for my work on a total thyroidectomy, a roughly 2-hour case. Was there an error, or was this to be considered "fair" compensation? Growing up, my brother and I operated on stuffed animals from time to time, once removing a broken windup music box to rescue an ailing teddy bear. But real surgery isn't such a crude undertaking. When it comes to resecting the entire thyroid gland, for example, there are numerous pitfalls, like damaging the nerves controlling the voice box, or devascularizing the tiny parathyroid glands which share the same blood supply. Any latent bleeding, on the other hand, might compromise the airway and the very life of the patient.

Insurance payment reports go by various names like "EOB" (Explanation of Benefits) or "RA" (Remittance Advice), and will frequently have so-called remark codes describing the particular determinations. The payment record for the thyroidectomy read "Charge exceeds fee schedule/maximum allowable or contracted/ legislated fee arrangement." I telephoned Cigna to ask just how this claim was paid, and the agent said "I show you having an open access plan...but no contract." The root meaning of the Greek word *oxymoron* is "sharp-dull," signifying a self-contradictory notion. Here, it would be something like "Your non-contracted claim was paid according to your contract."

Cigna's adjudication of this claim was emblematic of many to follow, and it became apparent that appealing by phone was fruitless. As a result I began to submit formal letters for these dubious remittances which prompted responses like the following for a laparoscopic cholecystectomy, removal of the gallbladder: "We have reviewed the claim in question and determined that, according to your contract, no additional payment is due. This claim was processed correctly per your Cigna OAP [Open Access Plus] fee schedule. According to your contract the allowance for procedure code 47562 is $686.68 x 16% = $109.87." I requested a copy of the purported contract, but none was produced.

Other claims were meanwhile being denied outright on such grounds as "Services not provided by network...provider[]." In the words of one patient whom I subsequently billed on Cigna's advice, "Because you're out-of-network, Cigna isn't paying anything." She, for one, hadn't been informed by Cigna of its policy designating assistant surgeons as "non-PAR."

Finding the status quo unacceptable I called Cigna once again in the effort to resolve exactly how these claims were being processed. An agent named Weylin said "As I pull our records, you're *not* contracted as a surgical assistant," yet acknowledged that most of the remittances made reference to a "fee schedule" or "contracted[] fee arrangement."

I submitted a final appeal letter addressing not just the index claim but "related issues": "[I]f the numerous seemingly encumbered, underpaid, and/or improperly denied claims...have simply been a matter of clerical error, I presently request a comprehensive review of all claims, with supplemental payments to be issued as indicated."

Cigna replied to the ultimatum mechanically: "After reviewing your request, we have decided to uphold the original decision [¶] ... [¶] This is the final internal level of appeal."

Chapter 3

I'd like to share a story from back when I was launching my former private practice. I received a year-end call from the accountant I had retained by referral but whom I otherwise didn't know all that well. It took me off guard when among a series of other questions he asked if there was any pending litigation. In the moment before I replied "No" I was thinking only unreasonable people end up in lawsuits, and so for him to ask if *my* practice was entangled in litigation, did he believe *I* was an unreasonable person? Perhaps I'm a little less naïve today. Along the way I've read (often listened to) a number of books, including *Shoe Dog* by Phil Knight, the founder of Nike, who concludes "business is war." But, who would step into the arena as my warrior against Cigna?

The regulatory agencies in California are regrettably like an edentulous rodent. I think I carried more authority on the Safety Patrol in the fifth grade than the California Department of Managed Health Care or Department of Insurance wield against insurance companies.

As to finding a champion in a lawyer, also problematic. I spoke to an attorney at a prominent healthcare law firm who graciously took my call but explained that even if I could handle the minimum rate of $630 per hour, they already represented clients like Cigna. For a time I did engage a smaller outfit but found their work to be inadequate, whether because of hollow pleadings or repeatedly missed or threatened deadlines.

And so proceeded in the Superior Court of the State of California for the County of Sacramento "John B Hackert, MD, *In pro per* v. Cigna Health and Life Insurance Company; Cigna Health Corporation; and Cigna Healthcare of California, Inc." The phrase *In pro per* is an abbreviation of Latin's *in propria persona*, which might be translated "in the person of yourself." An equivalent phrase, *pro se*, means "for himself." Abraham Lincoln is credited with the adage "He who represents himself has a fool for a client." But is not justice blind? I'm afraid the Yogi Berraism would be something like "The law is not lawful." This book is to some degree a You Be the Judge account. There will be frequent case citations,[1] many to the US Supreme Court itself, about which the illuminati of the law might chortle, "It *says* that, but it doesn't *mean* that!"

My complaint against Cigna in its final form alleged the following causes of action: Breach of Contract; Breach of Covenant of Good Faith and Fair Dealing; Negligent Misrepresentation; Quantum Meruit; Injunctive Relief; and Declaratory Relief.

Let me explain what my rationale was as a non-lawyer for each of these counts.

BREACH OF CONTRACT

Even though Cigna *said* there was no written contract, the remittance record was largely contrary. If Cigna's angle would be that the contract from my former practice continued despite the verbal representations of agents like Deedee and Weylin, my belief was that once this agreement surfaced through discovery, many of the claims would be found to be underpaid, certainly those where Cigna remitted nothing.

For some background on contracts, the California Supreme Court in *Marvin v. Marvin*, 18 Cal. 3d 660 (Cal. 1976) noted:

> Contracts may be express or implied. These terms however do not denote different kinds of contracts, but have reference to the evidence by which the agreement between the parties is shown. If the agreement is shown by the direct words of the parties, spoken or written, the contract is said to be an express one. But if such agreement can only be shown by the acts and conduct of the parties, interpreted in the light of the subject matter and of the surrounding circumstances, then the contract is an implied one. [I]n a sense all contracts made in fact, as distinguished from quasi-contractual obligations, are express contracts, differing only in the manner in which the assent of the parties is expressed and proved.

If the former written contract was terminated when Cigna's agent stated "You'll be considered non-PAR," an oral contract may have been created by "novation." The Ninth Circuit Court in *Fanucchi & Limi*

Farms v. United Agri Products, 414 F.3d 1075 (9th Cir. 2005) recognized that "Section 1698(b) [of the California Civil Code] allows modification of a written contract by an oral agreement to the extent the oral agreement is executed."

It's a maxim that both an offer and acceptance are required to form a contract, and there must also be mutual "consideration," exchange of something of value. Upon the announcement that I would become a "non-PAR," Cigna arguably extended an oral contract by which I would provide surgical assistant services to Cigna members in exchange for compensation. Acceptance was reflected by my later provision of these services and Cigna's payment, generally, for which, albeit at an amount contested.

Cigna's "position on reimbursing assistant surgeons" as published on its website noted that surgical assistant claims are identified by CPT (Current Procedural Terminology[2]) Modifier 80. A table specifying "Reimbursement per Assistant Surgeon Modifier" included a bulleted item "Modifier 80 - 16% of fee schedule or usual & customary/ maximum reimbursable rate."

A fee schedule is a listing of reimbursements a provider specifically agrees to under contract. By electing to participate in a network, the provider hopes to receive more patient referrals, but as a concession often accepts a lower rate than market. This is sometimes called "the PPO discount," where PPO stands for "Preferred Provider Organization."

How, though, is a "*non*-PAR" assistant surgeon to be reimbursed, at "16% of fee schedule" or "usual & customary/maximum reimbursable rate"? The convention of paying non-PAR providers at usual and customary in lieu of a written contract had appeared in caselaw, like *DEMARIA v. HORIZON HEALTHCARE SERVICES, INC.*, No. 11-7298 (WJM) (D.N.Y. June 1, 2015): "Non Par providers have no agreement with Horizon; instead, Horizon pays them for treating Horizon Insureds at 'usual and customary' rates."

BREACH OF COVENANT OF GOOD FAITH AND FAIR DEALING

"There is an implied covenant of good faith and fair dealing in every contract...." (*Comunale v. Traders & General Ins. Co.*, 50 Cal. 2d 654 (Cal. 1958).) "A party violates the covenant...if its conduct is objectively unreasonable." (*Carma Developers (Cal.), Inc. v. Marathon Development California, Inc.*, 2 Cal. 4th 342 (Cal. 1992).) "Breach of a specific provision of the contract is not a necessary prerequisite. Were it otherwise, the covenant would have no practical meaning, for any breach thereof would necessarily involve breach of some other term of the contract." (*Id.*)

The notation "*Id.*," by the way, is an abbreviation of the Latin word "idem," used to refer to the authority just cited.

If I were *provisionally* found to be under contract to accept 16% of a fee schedule I had no occasion to negotiate, such a contract was objectively unreasonable as one of "adhesion." The California Court of Appeal in *Discover Bank v. Superior Court*, 134 Cal. App. 4th 886 (Cal. App. 2d Dist. 2005) described a contract of adhesion as "drafted unilaterally by the dominant party and then presented on a 'take-it-or-leave-it' basis to the weaker party who has no real opportunity to bargain about its terms."

"Generally speaking, there are two judicially imposed limitations on the enforcement of adhesion contracts or provisions thereof. The first is that such a contract or provision which does not fall within the reasonable expectations of the weaker or 'adhering' party will not be enforced against him. The second, a principle of equity applicable to all contracts generally is that a contract or provision, even if consistent with the reasonable expectations of the parties, will be denied enforcement if, considered in its context, it is unduly oppressive or 'unconscionable.'" (*Graham v. Scissor-Tail, Inc.*, 28 Cal. 3d 807 (Cal. 1981).)

This cause of action sought to address another concern, that Cigna had been leasing access to my services to other entities like the rental network known as MultiPlan[3] at a discounted rate for an apparent commission, without my assent. This type of "silent PPO" contravenes California law (e.g., Insurance Code § 10178.3), and has been described by the courts as a "scheme...involv[ing] a payor who has an agreement with a network vendor and claims the discounted preferred provider organization rate for services but without providing any incentives to channel clients to that provider." (*UFCW & Employers Benefit Trust v. Sutter Health*, 241 Cal. App. 4th 909 (Cal. App. 1st Dist. 2015).)

Also germane to this Covenant of Good Faith cause, there were a handful of cases where the level of technical difficulty led the primary surgeon to append to the procedure codes Modifier 22, "Unusual

Procedural Services," which per industry standards calls for augmenting reimbursement by 20 percent. According to its own published policy, "Cigna may provide additional reimbursement for Modifier 22 up to a maximum of 120% of the appropriate fee schedule or maximum allowed fee when the documentation submitted adequately demonstrates substantially increased time and complexity compared to what is typically provided, and that such additional services cannot be billed with other more appropriate procedural codes." Even when I attached the operative reports—the "op notes"—to those claims, Cigna paid no more with "Mod" 22 than without.

NEGLIGENT MISREPRESENTATION

The California Supreme Court observed in *Applied Equipment Corp. v. Litton Saudi Arabia Ltd.*, 7 Cal. 4th 503 (Cal. 1994) that in contrast to contractual damages, "tort damages are awarded to compensate the victim for injury suffered. For the breach of an obligation not arising from contract, the measure of damages...is the amount which will compensate for all the detriment proximately caused thereby, whether it could have been anticipated or not.' (Civ. Code, § 3333.)"

"Negligent misrepresentation is a form of deceit, the elements of which consist of (1) a misrepresentation of a past or existing material fact, (2) without reasonable grounds for believing it to be true, (3) with intent to induce another's reliance on the fact misrepresented, (4) ignorance of the truth and justifiable reliance thereon by the party to whom the misrepresentation was directed, and (5) damages." (*Fox v. Pollack*, 181 Cal. App. 3d 954 (Cal. App. 1st Dist. 1986).)

Each of the so-called "elements" of this tort was present: (1) Cigna's agents represented "You will be considered non-PAR;" "You're *not* contracted as a surgical assistant." It was a material fact whether I was participating or non-participating because compensation was, apparently, "16% of fee schedule" for participating assistants under written contract, but "usual & customary" in the absence of a written contract. By a reasonable person standard (*Charpentier v. L.A. Rams Football Co.*, 75 Cal. App. 4th 301 (Cal. App. 4th Dist. 1999)) it was a *mis*representation that "[I] will be considered non-PAR" because Cigna had been reimbursing the claims at the participating rate of "16% of fee schedule," not the "usual & customary/maximum reimbursable rate." (2) There could be no reasonable grounds for Cigna to believe

11

that "[I] will be considered non-PAR" because Cigna continued to invoke contractual discounts. (3) Cigna must have intended to induce my reliance upon the misrepresented fact, as I otherwise would have had the opportunity during the call with agent Deedee to reconsider the terms of any written contract, including the option to formally terminate at that time so that payment might be "usual & customary" rather than "16% of fee schedule." Evidence of Cigna's intention to induce my reliance on the misrepresented fact was reflected by Cigna's refusal to remit corrective payments as the final appeal letter demanded. (4) I had been ignorant of the truth, that Cigna would continue to assert a contractual basis for reducing my reimbursement for surgical assistant services despite representing that "[I] will be considered non-PAR." As the California Supreme Court described in *Alliance Mortgage Co. v. Rothwell*, 10 Cal. 4th 1226 (1995), "Reliance exists when the misrepresentation or nondisclosure was an immediate cause of the plaintiff's conduct which altered his or her legal relations, and when without such misrepresentation or nondisclosure he or she would not, in all reasonable probability, have entered into the contract or other transaction." Taking into account my own education, experience, and knowledge at the time, my reliance upon Cigna's misrepresentation was reasonable. But for Cigna's misrepresentation that "[I] will be considered non-PAR," I would have had the opportunity to renegotiate or terminate the asserted written contract. (5) As a direct and proximate result of Cigna's negligent misrepresentation, I suffered damages represented by the difference between the estimated usual & customary rate and the actual payments for each of what were 32 separate claims at issue.

QUANTUM MERUIT

"Pleading alternative counts is appropriate when the plaintiff is certain of his or her legal rights but is in doubt about some of the ultimate facts, which may perhaps be largely within the knowledge of the defendant." (*State Compensation Insurance Fund v. NOTIS ENTERPRISES, INC.*, No. B213079 (Cal. Ct. App. June 7, 2010).)

Because it could be found as an "ultimate fact" that there was no contract in any form—written, oral, or otherwise—quantum meruit, Latin for "the amount earned," stood as an alternative cause of action:

> Quantum meruit refers to the well-established principle
> that the law implies a promise to pay for services

12

performed under circumstances disclosing that they were not gratuitously rendered. To recover in quantum meruit, a party need not prove the existence of a contract, but it must show the circumstances were such that the services were rendered under some understanding or expectation of both parties that compensation therefor was to be made. (*Huskinson & Brown v. Wolf*, 32 Cal. 4th 453 (Cal. 2004).)

Framed in the above, the complaint argued I provided surgical assistant services to Cigna members under the parties' expectation that compensation was to be made, as the services were not gratuitously rendered. There would be no way for Cigna to cover major surgical procedures without the involvement of an assistant surgeon, even if this medically necessary resource was ambiguously classified as "non-PAR."

Negotiation experts instruct that the value of a service executed on credit tends to rapidly decline once delivered, and this is often the paradigm of medical billing. If claims were to be reimbursed at a "usual & customary" rate, Cigna unilaterally determined that value retroactively. The series of appeal letters demanded that Cigna disclose how it calculated payment for the type of services provided, including market analysis, comparative data, and methodology, as well as what databases were relied upon. The "Ingenix" database, for one, had gained notoriety through a 2009 report by the United States Senate Committee on Commerce, Science, and Transportation:[4]

> Although the insurance industry represented the Ingenix data as accurate and objective, subsequent investigations have revealed that the reliability of the Ingenix data was fatally undermined by faulty statistical methods and a fundamental conflict of interest. [¶] ...[¶] The results of these questionable statistical methods were estimates of "usual and customary" charges that consistently skewed reimbursement rates downwards – in a direction that allowed insurers to reduce their claims payments. [¶ ... [¶] [A] statistical expert testified that insurance companies did not contribute complete sets of their medical claims data to Ingenix, and that some data contributors performed

13

"scrubs" that skewed the contributed data downwards. [¶] Once the contributed data arrived at Ingenix, the company employed yet another "scrubbing" process that again had the effect of inappropriately eliminating valid high charges from the database. [¶] ... [¶] [A]ll of the data Ingenix used to calculate its benchmark products came from the very same health insurers that purchased Ingenix's products, forming a "closed loop" of information between Ingenix and the insurance industry. Confidentiality agreements between Ingenix and its customers prohibited the disclosure of information about the database products to patients or doctors.

Some of the 32 claims at issue were of the HMO (Health Maintenance Organization) type, not PPO, and were thus governed by California's Knox Keene Act, a set of laws and statutes passed in 1975 to regulate HMO health care service plans.[5] It was my information that Cigna as the health care service plan retained liability for bariatric (i.e., weight loss) services under a "carveout" agreement with its intermediaries, medical practice groups which would otherwise have been responsible for reimbursing providers.[6] These HMO claims were subject to California Code of Regulations, title 28, section 1300.71, subdivision (a)(3) which reads:

> "Reimbursement of a Claim" means: (A) For contracted providers with a written contract...the agreed upon contract rate; (B) For contracted providers without a written contract and non-contracted providers, except those providing services described in paragraph (C) below: the payment of the reasonable and customary value for the health care services rendered based upon statistically credible information that is updated at least annually and takes into consideration: (i) the provider's training, qualifications, and length of time in practice; (ii) the nature of the services provided; (iii) the fees usually charged by the provider; (iv) prevailing provider rates charged in the general geographic area in which the services were rendered; (v) other aspects of the economics of the medical provider's practice that are

relevant; and (vi) any unusual circumstances in the case; and (C) For non-emergency services provided by non-contracted providers to PPO and POS enrollees: the amount set forth in the enrollee's Evidence of Coverage.

The California Department of Managed Health Care (DMHC) contemporaneously published the following:

The Knox-Keene Act's Regulations, Title 28, Section 1300.71(a)(3)(B), require payors to reimburse non-contracted providers in an amount equal to the reasonable and customary value of the service. In the past several years the DMHC has seen an increase in complaints from non-contracted providers concerning reasonable and customary value payments by payors. [¶] The DMHC considers the fair reimbursement of providers a serious issue....[7]

Existing caselaw fully accorded: "As recognized by the DMHC, section 1300.71(a)(3)(B)'s directive to pay noncontracted providers the reasonable and customary value of their services embodies the concept of quantum meruit." (*Children's Hospital Central California v. Blue Cross of California*, 226 Cal. App. 4th 1260 (Cal. App. 5th Dist. 2014).)

INJUNCTIVE RELIEF

"An injunction is a writ or order requiring a person to refrain from a particular act. It may be granted by the court in which the action is brought, or by a judge thereof; and when granted by a judge, it may be enforced as an order of the court." (California Code of Civil Procedure, or "CCP," section 525.)

CCP § 526 reads in part, "An injunction may be granted in the following cases: (1) When it appears by the complaint that the plaintiff is entitled to the relief demanded.... [¶] (3) When it appears, during the litigation, that a party to the action is doing, or threatens, or is about to do, or is procuring or suffering to be done, some act in violation of the rights of another party to the action.... [¶] (6) Where the restraint is necessary to prevent a multiplicity of judicial proceedings...."

California Business and Professions Code § 17200 *et seq.* (Latin for "and following"), also known as the Unfair Competition Law or

UCL, "provides in part: 'unfair competition shall mean and include any unlawful, unfair or fraudulent business act or practice....'" (*Madrid v. Perot Systems Corp.*, 130 Cal. App. 4th 440 (Cal. App. 3d Dist. 2005).)

My complaint asked the court to enjoin Cigna from violating the UCL and to order Cigna to pay future claims at the "usual & customary/maximum reimbursable rate."

DECLARATORY RELIEF

California Code of Civil Procedure section 1060 states "Any person...who desires a declaration of his or her rights or duties with respect to another...may, in cases of actual controversy relating to the legal rights and duties of the respective parties, bring an original action...in the superior court for a declaration of his or her rights and duties...."

Hand-in-hand with the request for injunctive relief, the complaint asked the court for a declaration of the parties' rights and responsibilities as to the controversy over Cigna's reimbursement of my surgical assistant services.

Chapter 4

A potential legal challenge the complaint sought to address upfront was the federal regulation known as "ERISA," the acronymic name for the Employee Retirement Income Security Act.[8]

You may have noticed the phrase "insurance company" is heard less and less in healthcare contexts. Cigna, for example, describes itself on its website as "a global health service company."[9] The word "insurance" appears only in the footer of their "About Us" page under a rubric reading "Disclaimer." The reason, I believe, is ERISA.

As the US Supreme Court rehearsed in *Pilot Life Ins. Co. v. Dedeaux*, 481 U.S. 41, 107 S. Ct. 1549, 95 L. Ed. 2d 39 (1987), "ERISA comprehensively regulates, among other things, employee welfare benefit plans that, through the purchase of insurance or otherwise, provide medical, surgical, or hospital care, or benefits in the event of sickness, accident, disability, or death."

ERISA has the capacity to "federally preempt," that is supplant, state law. A California appellate court boiled down this complex topic:

> The preemption language in ERISA has been well explored in a series of federal decisions. The language is structured in three parts. First there is a broad preemption clause, preempting state laws which "relate to any employee benefit plan." Then there is a "saving clause" which excludes any state law which "regulates insurance" from the scope of the preemption clause. Finally, there is a "deemer" clause which, as a practical matter, carves out an exception to the saving clause by providing that employee benefit plans shall not be "deemed" insurance companies for purposes of the saving clause. [¶] ... [¶] The key issue is whether the...plan is deemed an "insurance company." For better or worse, the test laid down by the United States Supreme Court on the application of the deemer clause is whether the particular plan in question is self-funded.

If so, the plan is governed by ERISA. (*Inter Valley Health Plan v. Blue Cross-Blue Shield*, 16 Cal. App. 4th 60 (Cal. App. 4th Dist. 1993).)

As will become evident as this book unfolds, at least larger employers, and their attorneys, seem to favor ERISA's federalizing effect. Picture a typical corporation. Most likely it will not offer "health insurance" to its employees but rather the "benefit" of healthcare. It will not purchase "insurance," but rather will pay a fee—not a "premium"—to a Cigna, for example, to act as its third-party administrator while self-funding the benefits.

When it comes to receiving actual health care, most patients would probably find it overwhelming to prepare and submit a claim to payers like Cigna for remuneration of their benefits. The culture in the US healthcare system is that after rendering services, the medical provider will file a claim to the payer in the patient's stead. This, by the way, is of course at the provider's expense, whether directly or indirectly through a billing service. With the exception of copayments or deductibles, the patient is theoretically left out of the fray.

The transference of a patient's healthcare benefits to the medical provider is most formally accomplished by an "Assignment of Benefits" form, which you may recall completing at a doctor's office yourself. But what if the provider, like the typical assistant surgeon, doesn't have the patient's express written assignment, and yet is expected to file a claim on the patient's behalf? Is such a provider the patient's assignee under ERISA?

The Ninth Circuit of the US Court of Appeals whose jurisdiction includes California found in *Misic v. Building Service Employees Health*, 789 F.2d 1374 (9th Cir. 1986) that a provider "stands in the shoes of the assignor...if the assignment is valid," but left undefined what makes for a "valid" assignment.

The Ninth Circuit did clarify that "ERISA's civil enforcement provision, 29 U.S.C. § 1132(a), identifies only plan participants, beneficiaries, fiduciaries, and the Secretary of Labor as '[p]ersons empowered to bring a civil action.' [A] non-participant health care provider...cannot bring claims for benefits on its own behalf. It must do so derivatively, relying on its patients' assignments of their benefits claims." (*Spinedex Physical Therapy USA v. United Healthcare*, 770 F.3d 1282 (9th Cir. 2014).)

"A 'fiduciary'," by the way, is defined as "an entity with 'any discretionary authority' in the 'administration of' an ERISA plan. 29 U.S.C. § 1002(21)(A)." (*Saffon v. Wells Fargo & Co. Long Term Disability*, 522 F.3d 863 (9th Cir. 2008).)

In anticipation of this ERISA quagmire my complaint plead that "[w]ith respect to any issue in this matter which may putatively be subject to federal preemption under the Employee Retirement Income Security Act ('ERISA'), plaintiff is not a fiduciary, beneficiary, or assignee of any beneficiary, but rather brings suit as an independent, third-party entity."

I cited the Ninth Circuit in *Cedars-Sinai Med. Ctr. v. NAT'L LEAG., POST., US*, 497 F.3d 972 (9th Cir. 2007) which found that "ERISA [*would*] preempt the state claims of a provider suing as an assignee of the beneficiary's rights to benefits under an ERISA plan[,¶ but] [h]ere, Cedars-Sinai is suing as a third-party claiming damages, and not as an assignee of rights to benefits." The complaint also cited a related Ninth Circuit decision, *The Meadows v. Employers Health Ins.*, 47 F.3d 1006 (9th Cir. 1995): "The question before us...is whether ERISA preempts claims by a third-party who sues an ERISA plan not as an assignee of a purported ERISA beneficiary, but as an independent entity claiming damages. We hold that ERISA does not."

Unfortunately though, sagacity of vision may not be sufficient to control what lies ahead of us.

Chapter 5

Upon receiving the summons the various Cigna defendants did select a champion, a law firm known then as Kennaday, Leavitt & Daponde PC. They apparently took the complaint seriously enough to retain a "Super Lawyer," partner Curtis Leavitt.[10] According to his published bio, Mr. Leavitt earned a Bachelor of Arts *summa cum laude* in Cell Biology and Physiology, a common pre-*medical* major, apparently suitable to healthcare law. The associate attorney initially assigned to the case, David McDonough, had a similar background in molecular biology before becoming barred. It's one of my cynical jokes, that there is money to be made in medicine, just not in its practice.

As an early maneuver, Cigna's medically versant legal team "removed" the case to federal court:

> Defendants CIGNA HEALTH AND LIFE INSURANCE COMPANY; CIGNA HEALTH CORPORATION; and CIGNA HEALTHCARE OF CALIFORNIA, INC., (collectively, "Cigna") hereby remove this action from the Superior Court of the State of California, County of Sacramento, to the United States District Court for the Eastern District of California, Sacramento Division, pursuant to Title 28, United States Code, sections 1441(a) and 1446. Removal is based on the original jurisdiction of the district court pursuant to Title 28, United States Code, section 1331 and Title 29, United States Code, section 1001, *et seq.* the Employee Retirement Income Security Act of 1974 ("ERISA").

Like Darth Vader warming up the tractor beam, the notice of removal pronounced, "Plaintiff cannot escape the complete preemptive force of ERISA...."

Chapter 6

Now in federal court Cigna's attorneys answered my complaint and filed a Counterclaim made up of this series of individual counterclaims:

(1) For recovery of overpayment of plan benefits under 29 U.S.C. § 1132(a)(3)
(2) Unjust Enrichment
(3) Constructive Trust
(4) Common Count, Money Had and Received

Of the 32 claims my complaint had alleged to be underpaid, Cigna's countersuit itemized 18 asserted overpayments. The counterclaim-at-large pled "[t]he amounts Cigna paid to Plaintiff for these services greatly exceeded the amounts Cigna was obligated to pay Plaintiff."

Reading the phrase "*greatly* exceeded" may cause a lawyer to salivate, while fans of the underdog might be expected to shudder, but I'm afraid the next passage will underwhelm: "Cigna has preliminarily calculated its overpayments to Plaintiff at approximately $2,980.41."

Of course Cigna would've already had to pay these attorneys well over 3K just to pull them off the scent of other quarry, and it was my impression from the outset that the counterclaim was meritless and designed to intimidate me into dropping the case.

Like a saber rattled a little too loudly, the cross-complaint went on to threaten that "overpayments and interest on those overpayments, are continuing to accrue as Plaintiff treats more Cigna Members, and Cigna continues to locate overpaid claims."

Get out of our sandbox or else.

Chapter 7

In response to the notice of removal I filed a motion to "remand," arguing on two independent points that the case should be returned to state court:

> (1) The district court lacks subject matter jurisdiction because plaintiff is not an assignee of any beneficiary vis-à-vis ERISA; and
>
> (2) Plaintiff's state-law cause of action of negligent misrepresentation is not federally preempted under ERISA

"The United States Code," abbreviated U.S.C., "is a consolidation and codification by subject matter of the general and permanent laws of the United States."[11] My motion to remand cited in part 28 U.S.C. § 1447(c) which states "If at any time before final judgment it appears that the district court lacks subject matter jurisdiction, the case shall be remanded."

I attached to the motion the following declaration in standard format:

> 1. I, John B Hackert M.D., declare the following to be my own personal knowledge, except as to those matters set forth on information and belief, and as to those matters, I believe them to be true, and if called upon to testify, could competently testify thereto.
> 2. I am the plaintiff in the above-referenced matter.
> 3. I am not a fiduciary, beneficiary, or assignee of any beneficiary of any CIGNA patient vis-à-vis ERISA.
> 4. Specifically, I do not have any assignment of benefits on file for any CIGNA patient, written or otherwise.
> 5. I have historically utilized a billing service for submission of claims to CIGNA.
> 6. Although the claim submission protocols of my

25

former or current billing services may potentially suggest that there was assignment of benefits, no actual assignment of benefits exists for any of the claims I have submitted to CIGNA through the agency of a billing service, or otherwise.

In addition to re-citing *Cedars-Sinai Med. Ctr.*, *The Meadows*, and *Misic*, I pointed out that "[t]he burden of establishing federal jurisdiction is on the party seeking removal, and the removal statute is strictly construed against removal jurisdiction." (*Prize Frize, Inc. v. Matrix (US) Inc.*, 167 F.3d 1261 (9th Cir. 1999).)

I extensively quoted *Hobbs v. Blue Cross Blue Shield of Alabama*, 276 F.3d 1236 (11th Cir. 2001) which reversed the lower court's denial of a similar motion to remand. There, Blue Cross was the "claims administrator of [an ERISA] plan" and sought to remove the state-court action of plaintiffs who were physician assistants seeking damages related to the provision of medical services. Blue Cross argued that "the [district] court had federal question jurisdiction because the state law claim set forth in the complaint was completely preempted under ERISA." The Eleventh Circuit reasoned, however, that "[u]nder the doctrine of complete preemption, a plaintiff must have standing to sue under a relevant ERISA plan before a state law claim can be recharacterized as arising under federal law, subject to federal court jurisdiction," noting that "[t]he only parties that have standing to sue under ERISA are those listed in the civil enforcement provision of ERISA"—a "participant" or "beneficiary." Blue Cross maintained that plaintiffs Hobbs and Irvine had standing under ERISA because they were "seeking benefits as *purported* assignees of their patients' benefits under ERISA-governed Blue Cross plans," that is "derivative standing." The court observed nevertheless that it "has allowed healthcare providers to use derivative standing to sue under ERISA...only...when the healthcare provider had obtained a *written* assignment of claims from a patient." (Emphasis added.) The Eleventh concluded that "Hobbs and Irvine do not have standing to present an ERISA claim because they are not participants or beneficiaries in an employee health care plan. Blue Cross failed to demonstrate that Hobbs and Irvine had standing based on an assignment of their patients' claims and benefits. Thus, this matter was improperly removed to federal court because it did not have subject matter

26

jurisdiction."

I argued Cigna's removal was likewise improper here because I was not a beneficiary or assignee of any beneficiary vis-à-vis ERISA, and thus the district court lacked subject matter jurisdiction. The "vis-à-vis" qualifier, incidentally, was not an attempt at loquacious legalese but rather clarification that I was not an assignee *as contemplated by ERISA*: I had not "obtained a *written* assignment of claims from a[ny] patient."

To illustrate that my cause of negligent misrepresentation was not federally preempted, I cited *Franciscan Skemp Healthcare, Inc. v. Central States Joint Bd. Health and Welfare Trust Fund*, 538 F.3d 594 (7th Cir. 2008). There, plaintiff-appellant Franciscan was a healthcare provider. The defendant-appellee, Central States, was an employee benefit plan. Sherry Romine was a Central States plan participant through her employment. Franciscan brought suit against Central States alleging, in part, negligent misrepresentation based upon Central States refusal to pay for medical services after representing that Romine was covered for those services. By reference to the US Supreme Court's "Davila test" from *Aetna Health Inc. v. Davila*, 542 U.S. 200, 124 S. Ct. 2488, 159 L. Ed. 2d 312 (2004), the Eighth Circuit remanded the case:

> Franciscan Skemp is bringing these claims of negligent misrepresentation and estoppel, not as Romine's assignee, but entirely in its own right. These claims arise not from the plan or its terms, but from the alleged oral representations made by Central States to Franciscan. [¶]...[¶] Franciscan...seeks damages, not wrongfully denied benefits. [¶] Therefore, under the first consideration from *Davila*, the claims are not preempted because they could not have been brought under ERISA § 502(a)(1)(B). [¶] Franciscan Skemp is not suing "to recover benefits due...under the terms of [the] plan, to enforce...rights under the terms of the plan, or to clarify...rights to future benefits under the terms of the plan," which is precisely all § 502(a)(1)(B) provides. Franciscan...is seeking damages arising from alleged misrepresentations made by Central States to Franciscan...in response to its inquiry—a wrong not

within § 502's scope. [¶] Analysis under the second step in the Davila test—whether there is an independent legal duty implicated by the defendant's actions—also undercuts finding the claims completely preempted. The claims of negligent misrepresentation and estoppel derive from duties imposed apart from ERISA and/or the plan terms....

I argued that removal was improper here because, in the same way, Cigna's misrepresentation was a wrong not within § 502's scope. Placed in context, Cigna said I would be considered non-PAR, and non-PAR providers are, apparently, to be reimbursed at usual & customary value, thus Cigna should be estopped—prevented—from retrospectively imposing the terms of ERISA plans on the services I had already provided in reliance on their characterization.

I concomitantly filed a motion to dismiss their federal counterclaims, citing in part the US Supreme Court:

The objection that a federal court lacks subject-matter jurisdiction, see Fed. Rule Civ. Proc.[12] 12(b)(1), may be raised by a party, or by a court on its own initiative, at any stage in the litigation, even after trial and the entry of judgment. Rule 12(h)(3) instructs: "Whenever it appears by suggestion of the parties or otherwise that the court lacks jurisdiction of the subject matter, the court shall dismiss the action." (*Arbaugh v. Y & H Corp.*, 546 U.S. 500, 126 S. Ct. 1235, 163 L. Ed. 2d 1097 (2006).)

The question of course was how my suggestion would appear to the eyes of the district court.

Chapter 8

It's the classic instruction to the multiple choice test-taker: "mark the *best* answer." Sometimes there may seem to be competing answers, or no *good* answer at all, but you need to make your selection. Submitting claims for medical services isn't much different. No, you can't just send a postcard to Cigna saying "this is the work I did for this particular patient on this particular date, kindly remit payment." Instead there's a standardized claim submission format, whether the paper version known as the "CMS 1500" form[13] after the Centers for Medicare & Medicaid Services, or an electronic equivalent of which.

Box 27 of the CMS 1500 reads "ACCEPT ASSIGNMENT?," and the choices are "YES" or "NO." Responding "No" would necessarily duplicate the billing overhead to a practice, because a claim must first be submitted to the payer which will issue any payment to the patient, to whom another "claim" must be submitted—a bill—if the physician hopes to ultimately receive compensation for the services provided. Moreover, not as an editorial but a simple reality, some patients are not inclined to forward insurance payments on to their providers, involving yet another ungraceful layer, collections.

Box 13 of the CMS 1500 reads, "INSURED'S OR AUTHORIZED PERSON'S SIGNATURE [¶] I authorize payment of medical benefits to the undersigned physician or supplier for services described below." Billing services will stamp "SIGNATURE ON FILE" into this box, as patients historically have not been expected to apply their wet signature to the claim forms a provider is submitting for them, and the trend toward electronic submission would become an impossibility otherwise. Notably absent from the CMS 1500 is a checkbox indicating that the claim is being submitted on the patient's behalf *without* signaturized assignment of benefits.

Caselaw is not encyclopedic, by which I mean issues are heard and decided in a given venue only as they come. As a result an "on point" citation might only be found out-of-circuit or out-of-state, and thus considered "persuasive" but not necessarily "binding" locally. The Eleventh Circuit did happen to address the assignment conundrum in *Klay v. All Defendants*, 389 F.3d 1191 (11th Cir. 2004): "When a patient receives care from an out-of-network physician, the physician can attempt to receive payment directly from the [plan] as a courtesy to the patient or the physician can receive a direct assignment of the patient's contractual right to reimbursement from the [plan]. Because the treating physician does not participate in the patient's plan, such claims for reimbursement are referred to as 'non-par' claims."

Although I would seem to have been submitting claims "as a courtesy to the patients" without "*direct* assignment," Cigna's counsel filed an opposition to my motion to remand insisting "Plaintiff <u>must</u> be proceeding as an assignee" (emphasis in original), relying on an affidavit of a Cigna Claims Service Analyst by the name of Cheri Baron who declared "The letter 'Y' next to the 'ASSIGN BENS:' field indicates that the medical claim was submitted under an assignment to Plaintiff of the member's rights under the health plan."

As to my position that the negligent misrepresentation cause was not preempted, Cigna argued "the Cigna Reimbursement Policies attached to the [complaint] both state emphatically on the first page that they were meant to 'supplement certain standard Cigna benefit plans,' but that the terms contained in a member's actual health benefit plan '***always supersedes*** the information in a reimbursement policy.'" The heavy emphasis suggested I touched a nerve. But the very point was that the plan documents need not be consulted if a non-PAR provider is to be reimbursed at usual & customary rates as in *DEMARIA, supra* (Latin for "[see] above" used in legal writings).

If such phrases as "usual & customary" or "reasonable & customary" are not familiar you might wonder what all the fuss is about. After all, there's been no mention of *un*usual or *un*reasonable or *un*customary reimbursement. What it comes down to is that plan documents and fee schedules tend to heavily discount the would-be market value of medical services. To a payer, "reasonable" compensation is *inordinate*.

When my motions to remand and dismiss came to hearing, among other Findings and Recommendations the assigned Magistrate Judge, Carolyn K. Delaney, issued the following:

> In determining whether ERISA preempts plaintiff's

claims, the court uses a two-prong test. See Aetna Health Inc. v. Davila, 542 U.S. 200, 210 (2004). A state law cause of action is completely preempted if (1) an individual, at some point in time, could have brought the claim under ERISA and (2) no other independent legal duty is implicated by defendant's actions. See Marin General Hospital v. Modesto & Empire Traction Company, 581 F.3d 941, 946 (9th Cir. 2009). As an assignee of plaintiff's patients, plaintiff has sought reimbursement for medical services provided to his patients. See Affidavit of Cheri Baron, ¶ 6 (ECF No. 12-1). Plaintiff could therefore have brought his claims under ERISA. See Blue Cross v. Anesthesia Care Associates Medical Group, Inc., 187 F.3d 1045, 1051 (9th Cir. 1999). With respect to the second prong, plaintiff contends that his claim for negligent misrepresentation is not federally preempted under ERISA. Plaintiff alleges that there was no agreement regarding reimbursement between the parties and that his claim for reimbursement is predicated on general reimbursement policies he downloaded from defendant's website. The exhibits plaintiff has attached to his second amended complaint state that "an individual's benefit plan document **always supercedes** [sic] the information in a reimbursement policy." ECF No. 1-12 at pp. 27, 33 (emphasis in original). Because the reimbursement policy on which plaintiff relies on its face requires an analysis of the underlying ERISA health benefit plans, plaintiff's negligent misrepresentation claim is not independent of ERISA. This action was therefore properly removed. (Emphasis in original. Fn omitted.)

I'm not sure I've come across a more tortured opinion than "As an assignee of plaintiff's patients, plaintiff has sought reimbursement for medical services provided to his patients." Are magistrate judges in such short supply that courts will settle for even the solecistic? No, I fear that phrase was deliberately contorted by its rather accomplished author, a graduate of Stanford Law School.[14] Surely Magistrate Judge

Delaney was capable of more straightforward sentence construction. A joke comes to mind, "What's the only composition course legal professionals are required to take?," and the punch line would be "Creative writing!"

As permitted I filed objections to the magistrate judge's Findings and Recommendations, including, among other points, a compelling citation to *GUERRIERE v. AETNA HEALTH, INC.*, Case No: 8: 07-cv-1440-T-23EAJ (M.D. Fla. Nov. 8, 2007): "[R]emoval statutes are construed narrowly; where plaintiff and defendant clash about jurisdiction, uncertainties are resolved in favor of remand."

Somewhat belatedly the assigned district court judge, Kimberly J. Mueller, carried out a self-described *de novo* analysis—Latin for "from new" as in "from the top." Judge Mueller found as to the question of subject matter jurisdiction that "Cigna's records show those claims were submitted under an assignment of rights," referencing *Spring E.R., LLC v. Aetna Life Ins. Co.*, No. 09-2001, 2010 WL 598748 (S.D. Tex. Feb. 17, 2010), a case Cigna had cited in its opposition erroneously as "*Spring E.R., LLC v. Cigna Life Insurance Co*, 2010 WL 598748, *3 (S.D. Tex. Feb. 17, 2010)." An early clue that the court was going to be smoothing things over for Goliath. To be sure the obverse *Hobbs* decision I had cited was out of circuit, but so was *Spring E.R.* where "whether Plaintiff received an assignment of the benefits under the ERISA plans" was also "fiercely disputed by the parties." The *Spring E.R.* plaintiffs pointed out that "[t]here is no assignment of benefits form even available at any of [our] emergency facilities" but the defendant insurance company produced claim forms from Spring E.R. on which the letter "Y" appeared in the assignment of benefits field. Contrary to *Hobbs* which called for evidence of *written* assignment, the *Spring E.R.* court concluded "[t]he possibility of direct payment is enough to establish subject matter jurisdiction" and denied Spring E.R.'s motion to remand.

Judge Mueller ruled that "Cigna has carried its burden to show Hackert submitted claims as his patients' assignee."

For the supposed sake of "judicial economy, convenience, and fairness to the litigants," Cigna had also asked the district court to exercise *supplemental* jurisdiction over certain of the claims Cigna itself identified as non-ERISA and therefore otherwise under state, not federal, jurisdiction. Per the Baron declaration, four of the thirty-two claims were "fully insured by Cigna," not self-funded. The US Supreme Court had determined that "employee benefit plans that are insured are subject to indirect state insurance regulation. [¶] ... [¶] [ERISA's] saving clause returns to the States the power to enforce those state laws that 'regulat[e] insurance[]'." (*FMC Corp. v. Holliday*, 498 U.S. 52, 111 S. Ct. 403, 112 L. Ed. 2d 356 (1990).)

Baron had also declared that "two claims...do not involve ERISA benefit plans, [as] the members were covered by their workers' union health plan, whereby Cigna priced the claim for the union plan, but did not pay it," namely that of the American Postal Workers Union or APWU.

Judge Mueller granted Cigna's request for supplemental jurisdiction despite my opposition and appropriate concern that for these non-ERISA claims the district court would whitewash state authority.

In what would become a common pattern, there was no discussion whatsoever of an entire point, the preemptability of the negligent misrepresentation cause of action, one of many tacit victories to come for Cigna.

Chapter 9

Amidst the pleadings on the motion to remand Cigna also amended its cross-complaint, expanding the individual counterclaims to include Fraud; Negligent Misrepresentation; and Unfair Competition in Violation of Business and Professions Code §§ 17200, *et seq*.

Even though my complaint, albeit "unverified" (that is, unsworn), had *already* proclaimed that I was not an assignee, perhaps Cigna's attorneys mustered these additional counterclaims because I had now formally *declared* via the motion to remand that I was "not a[n]...assignee." Or perhaps it was meant to be another turn of the screw because I hadn't yet folded.

These additional counterclaims alleged, as a family, that "Plaintiff enacted a scheme whereby Plaintiff submitted claims to Cigna for health care services rendered to Cigna Members and continually and repeatedly misrepresented to Cigna that Plaintiff had received assignments of benefits from the Cigna Members" which "fraudulently induces Cigna to pay claims." There must be "disgorgement" of these "ill-gotten gains," Cigna urged.

The section of the cross-complaint titled "FACTUAL ALLEGATIONS RELATED TO COUNTERCLAIMS" was unchanged in the amended version, still asserting the same 18 overpayments totaling $2,980.41. However each of the new fraud-centered counterclaims contended that "Cigna has been damaged" in the amount of "$23,330.83," a figure unaccompanied by any level of requisite "specificity" and "particularity"—compare Fed. Rule Civ. Proc. 9(b): "In alleging fraud[], a party must state with particularity the circumstances constituting fraud...."

Pleading deficiencies aside, the fraud allegations would seem to have become moot because Cigna had just argued that "Plaintiff <u>must</u> be proceeding as an assignee" and the judge found in its favor: "Hackert submitted claims as his patients' assignee." It would be incongruous to posit that I *had* assignment as plaintiff but *lacked* assignment as counterdefendant for the very same series of claims.

As the next step I answered the amended counterclaim and invoked my right to a jury:

> Plaintiff in this matter hereby demands a jury trial pursuant to Fed. R. Civ. P. 38, which states: "RIGHT PRESERVED. The right of trial by jury as declared by the Seventh Amendment to the Constitution—or as provided by a federal statute—is preserved to the parties inviolate."

Chapter 10

Sarcasm to me isn't necessarily a sign of a bitter heart but a form of humor. When facing an unpleasantry I often hear the voice of Rocky the Flying Squirrel from *The Adventures of Rocky and Bullwinkle*: "And now here's something we hope you'll *really* like...."

A sentiment fitting enough for a deposition? When I arrived at Kennaday, Leavitt & Daponde for the occasion I was introduced to Mr. Leavitt and a new associate attorney, Ms. Jennifer Nguyen, who had taken over from Mr. McDonough as a result of an apparent schism in the firm. I got the impression it was supposed to be Counselor Nguyen's stage with the partner in the supporting role, but Mr. Leavitt took more and more control over the depo until it morphed from the traditional Q & A format into almost a dialogue. "You have a fight in you!" he observed with what seemed a genuine smile.

It is of course the deponent who's supposed to yield information during these things, but I learned from Mr. Leavitt that he himself had been the author of the aforementioned California Code of Regulations, title 28, § 1300.71(a)(3) as former Assistant Chief Counsel to the Department of Managed Health Care. "I wrote it!!," he exclaimed when the topic arose.

In statutory interpretation the phrase "plain reading" carries an almost pejorative sense, as if the wording of a law is not to be trusted on its face and can be dependably construed by the judiciary alone. The culture seemed to be that section 1300.71(a)(3)(B) applied only to *emergency* services, even though its text and context in no way state that. I asked Mr. Leavitt whether the DMHC intended (a)(3)(B) to exclude elective services, and either out of pride or goodwill he answered with a simple "No!" and a still broader smile, as if to acknowledge the unnecessary controversy surrounding that regulation.

By way of the deposition I also came to possess what may have been an unintended second side of a "sword," a spreadsheet Cigna and attorneys had compiled and introduced into the record as an exhibit, including, remarkably, their own notes on each claim. Among other potential concessions, this document identified a MultiPlan discount on four of the claims, yet nonpayment on others. Which was it? If Cigna felt there was an agreement after all, then why were some claims denied? No provider would accept a contract without compensation, even if it were enforceable. If Cigna held to its apparent position that I was non-PAR, it exposed itself for colluding with MultiPlan's silent PPO racket. California Insurance Code § 10178.3(a), for example, states "In order to prevent the improper selling, leasing, or transferring of a health care provider's contract, it is the intent of the Legislature that every arrangement that results in a payor paying a health care provider a reduced rate for health care services based on the health care provider's participation in a network or panel shall be disclosed to the provider in advance...."

Later on in the process the parties would exchange various discovery demands, like requests for production of documents, interrogatories, and requests for admission—tools for impeachment when a party may later attempt to "change the story." And a big part of this story was going to change.

Chapter 11

Cigna next moved for summary judgment against my complaint "on the grounds that there are no genuine issues as to any material fact and Defendants are entitled to judgment as a matter of law."

In my effort to oppose this attempt to thwart a trial by jury, I noted that "the purpose of summary judgment is to avoid unnecessary trials when there is *no* dispute as to the facts before the court. The moving party is entitled to summary judgment as a matter of law where, viewing the evidence and the inferences arising therefrom in favor of the *non*movant, there are no genuine issues of material fact in dispute. When reasonable minds *could* differ on the material facts at issue, summary judgment is not appropriate." (*Northwest Motorcycle Ass'n v. USDA*, 18 F.3d 1468 (9th Cir. 1994). Emphasis added.)

Black's Law Dictionary, the standard, lists in paraphrase the following three definitions of the potentially ambiguous word "fact": (1) something that *actually* exists; (2) an *alleged* event or circumstance; and, more distantly, (3) an evil deed, as in "accessory after the fact." The English verb "to probe" is a cognate of Latin's *probare*, the gerundive of which is *probandum*, defined by Black's as "a fact *to be proved*." In the opposition I invoked the words of the Ninth Circuit: "[W]e do not necessarily assume the truth of legal conclusions merely because they are cast in the form of factual allegations." (*Paulsen v. CNF, Inc.*, 559 F.3d 1061, 1071 (9th Cir. 2009).) The key *probandum* in Cigna's motion for summary judgment was the assignment status. Cigna argued I had assignment, whereas I declared I didn't. Could not the minds of reasonable jurors differ on this question? It had become clear that the district court was partial to Cigna and its attorneys, but how best to confront a prejudiced bench? I decided to strategically quote prior decisions of Judge Mueller herself, like *LEXINGTON INSURANCE COMPANY v. ENERGETIC LATH & PLASTER, INC.*, No. 2: 15-cv-00861-KJM-EFB (E.D. Cal. Aug. 31, 2016), which included the insight that "competent testimony by a single declarant may defeat summary judgment though opposed by many other declarants" and "[t]he evidence of the non-movant is to be believed, and all justifiable inferences are to be drawn in . . . [the] [non-movant's] favor."

I just about needed an antiemetic whenever I read Cigna's pleadings, especially their memorandum and declarations in support of their MSJ. Just one of many so-stated "undisputed" facts laid out by Cigna was that "Hackert did not notify Cigna of his intent to provide 'assistant surgeon' services to the 32 Cigna members," which I naturally contested, referencing the telephone call with Deedee at provider relations. Cigna in its reply objected in turn that "The statements were allegedly made by a Cigna employee who has not been identified or made available for cross-examination."

Another Cigna employee, a Compliance Senior Specialist by the name of Emily Russell, simultaneously declared with "personal knowledge" that "Cigna told Dr. Hackert he was a 'non-participating' or 'noncontracted' provider. Though Dr. Hackert knew he was a non-contracted Cigna provider, Dr. Hackert nonetheless provided 'assistant surgeon' services to the 32 Cigna members."

You may wonder how Emily Russell had *personal* knowledge that Cigna told me I was non-participating, especially when they concomitantly argued that the employee who made that statement was not even "identified." Another inconsistency was that two of the patients in question had an additional procedure at a later time, and thus although I had tabulated 32 *claims* in my complaint, only 30 *patients* were involved.

Russell undersigned her declaration as follows: "I declare under penalty of perjury under the laws of the United States of America that the foregoing is true and correct." Of course any insightful judge could discern that this declaration could not have been made on personal knowledge, but I've been told such testimony "happens all the time."

You may be familiar with the catchphrase "Just the facts, ma'am" ascribed to the television show *Dragnet*. Sadly, though, the legal version would be "Anything *but* the facts ma'am!"

Chapter 12

As Cigna's motion for summary judgment came before Magistrate Judge Delaney, among other perfunctory references she quoted the Supreme Court in *Anderson v. Liberty Lobby, Inc.*, 477 U.S. 242, 106 S. Ct. 2505, 91 L. Ed. 2d 202 (1986): "In resolving the summary judgment motion, the evidence of the opposing party is to be believed." She then tucked the following contrariety into a footnote: "On the motion to remand, plaintiff asserted that he was not an assignee, an assertion expressly rejected by the District Court. In the opposition, plaintiff does not contest that he brings his claims as an assignee."

To appreciate the court's flagrancy, let me explain that the party opposing a motion for summary judgment must admit or deny every "undisputed" fact presented by the moving party, and Cigna had proffered "these bills state that Hackert received assignment of benefits from the 32 Cigna members." Despite the magistrate judge's account, here's how the opposition actually read:

> *Denied.* In the affidavit filed in support of his Motion to Remand, Hackert declared "I do not have any assignment of benefits on file for any CIGNA patient...."
>
> "These bills" referenced by [this Undisputed Fact] do not actually "state that Hackert received assignment of benefits," but simply indicate that Hackert was submitting claims on behalf of the given patients. It is considered standard in the healthcare industry for providers to submit claims on behalf of patients in this manner. This protocol is reflected in many of the plan documents[]: "How To File Your Claim [¶] Out-of-Network claims can be submitted by the provider if the provider is able and willing to file on your behalf."

Not included in Delaney's Findings and Recommendations, the *Anderson* court had also instructed that "Credibility determinations, the weighing of the evidence, and the drawing of legitimate inferences from the facts are jury functions, not those of a judge." But by "expressly rejecting" my declaration that I did not have assignment, Magistrate Judge Delaney not only weighed but *dis*believed key evidence from the opposing party, thus usurping the role of a jury.

Delaney "analyzed" the remaining issues at summary judgment in a similarly skewed, pro forma fashion. Cigna had contended "Because Hackert is seeking to recover benefits under these ERISA self-funded plans, his exclusive remedy was to file a claim under ERISA section 502(a), something Hackert elected not to do." I countered it was not by election but irrelevance that I had omitted a section 502(a) claim because, as pled, I did not consider myself to have assignment as of its writing. With the district court having since decided that "Cigna...carried its burden to show Hackert submitted claims as his patients' assignee," I observed in the opposition that "the Supreme Court has determined that the civil enforcement provision of ERISA 'completely preempts state law claims that come within its scope and *converts* these state claims into federal claims under § 502.'" (*Rose v. HealthCOMP, INC.*, No. 1: 15-cv-00619-SAB (E.D. Cal. Aug. 10, 2015). Emphasis added.) Magistrate Judge Delaney did not concur: "Plaintiff contends that his state law claims were automatically converted to a claim under section 502. This contention is simply unsupported in the case law."

Anticipating this conclusion, my opposition also sought leave to *amend* the complaint, supported by the Delaney-Mueller case *Bischoff v. Brittain*, No. 2: 14-cv-01970-KJM-CKD (E.D. Cal. May 2, 2016), reading:

> Federal Rule of Civil Procedure 15(a)(2) provides that "[t]he court should freely give leave [to amend [a] pleading] when justice so requires," and the Ninth Circuit has "stressed Rule 15's policy of favoring amendment[.] In exercising its discretion [regarding granting or denying leave to amend,] 'a court must be guided by the underlying purpose of Rule 15—to facilitate decision on the merits rather than on the pleadings or technicalities.'"

Delaney nevertheless made the determination that "[A]mendment would be futile. Plaintiff failed to exhaust the appeals procedures prescribed under the plans," suggesting by another footnote that I had submitted no more than "a single appeal letter."

Whether the magistrate judge was manufacturing the record or simply ignoring it, Cigna's *own* pleadings had itemized *six* appeal letters, including as an exhibit to the Russell Declaration my final correspondence which addressed not only that *particular* claim but "*related* issues." My opposition recapped that I had made *several* phone calls to Cigna in addition to issuing *numerous* appeal letters, including the last which demanded "a comprehensive review of *all* claims." I argued that Cigna was thus equitably estopped from asserting a failure to exhaust administrative remediation because they had refused the audit. "The court," Delaney proclaimed through yet another footnote, "finds no basis on the record before it for equitable estoppel."

Regarding the state-law causes of action for the remaining non-ERISA claims, Delaney parroted Cigna's fleshless and conclusory "argument" that "as to each claim, plaintiff cannot establish an essential element," ruling that "The undisputed facts establish that defendants' contention is well taken."

It was in one more footnote that the magistrate judge looked to the future of the case: "In the event that these findings and recommendations are adopted by the District Judge, the case will proceed to trial solely on the first amended counterclaim."

Chapter 13

Through his satire *Bleak House*, Charles Dickens long ago admonished against the fallacy that is law:

> This is the Court of Chancery, which has its decaying houses and its blighted lands in every shire, which has its worn-out lunatic in every madhouse and its dead in every churchyard, which...so exhausts finances, patience, courage, hope, so...breaks the heart, that there is not an honourable man among its practitioners who would not give--who does not often give--the warning, "Suffer any wrong that can be done you rather than come here!"

But having now stepped within "the walls of high Rome" (see Virgil's *Aeneid* I 1.7), my only path was to continue on according to the system—to keep playing the game by its rules, whether or not on a level field.

I thus filed objections to Delaney's Findings and Recommendations, even though Judge Mueller would surely rubberstamp them. Now I had to adopt a strategy of "preservation"— protection of the record for future appeal. Left unchallenged, insinuations such that I had filed merely "a single appeal letter" would effectively become "facts" of the case, and ultimately such "established" facts would be built into the highly emphasized pretrial order. Raising an issue only after the court has entered proposed findings of fact and conclusions of law limits appellate review in at least the Ninth Circuit according to such decisions as *Hotel Emp., et al. Health Tr. v. ELKS LODGE, 1450*, 827 F.2d 1324 (9th Cir. 1987).

My objections therefore reiterated the important factual disputes and legal issues, referencing additional authority as appropriate, like the Ninth Circuit's *McCartin v. Norton*, 674 F.2d 1317 (9th Cir. 1982): "Amendment is to be liberally granted where from the underlying facts or circumstances, the plaintiff may be able to state a claim."

Regarding the non-ERISA claims, I reviewed the merits of the state-law causes of action and the previously cited dispositive cases which had received no treatment by the magistrate judge. Considering these four claims were under *supplemental*, not actually federal, jurisdiction, the California law already cited should have been sufficient, but I now invoked some on-point federal cases like *MEDICAL AND CHIRURGICAL v. Aetna US Healthcare*, 221 F. Supp. 2d 618 (D. Md. 2002): "Plaintiffs assert that Defendants failed to comply with Maryland statutes that require HMOs to pay non-contracting physicians according to certain formulas... [i.e.,] the 'usual, customary, and reasonable' rate charged for the particular medical service.... While Defendants have paid Plaintiffs for their medical services, it has been at a rate below the rate dictated by those statutory formulas. In addition to bringing a cause of action under the statutes themselves, Plaintiffs assert claims...under a theory of quantum meruit. [¶] ... [¶] Plaintiffs are asserting in this action an independent statutory right of health care providers to receive payment consistent with the statutory formulas, not the right to any benefits due to plan participants. [¶] What is at issue is the amount of payment, and the source for that determination is the statutes, not the HMO plans."

Because granting the motion for summary judgment would displace the demanded jury, I looked to the US Supreme Court for refuge: "Maintenance of the jury as a fact-finding body is of such importance and occupies so firm a place in our history and jurisprudence that any seeming curtailment of the right to a jury trial should be scrutinized with the utmost care." (*Beacon Theatres, Inc. v. Westover*, 359 U.S. 500, 79 S. Ct. 948, 3 L. Ed. 2d 988 (1959).)

Lastly I sought to defend the ostensible right to a fair tribunal by advising recusal of Magistrate Judge Delaney: "A judge is required to disqualify himself in any proceeding in which his impartiality might reasonably be questioned and in proceedings where he has a personal bias or prejudice concerning a party. 28 U.S.C. § 455. Disqualification is required if a reasonable person with knowledge of all the facts would conclude that the judge's impartiality might reasonably be questioned." (*DEV v. Donahoe*, No. 14-15431 (9th Cir. Sept. 16, 2016).)

Chapter 14

In reply to my objections to the magistrate judge's advice regarding the motion for summary judgment, Cigna wrote "Hackert opposes the Findings and Recommendations. But his objections consist largely of rambling and conjecture, and reassert the following arguments which have already been rejected[, including that] Hackert is not an assignee of the claims at issue...." Like any well crafted lawyerspeak, some disassembly is required, but if I can carry the double negative in my head (one "rejected" cancels one "not"), Cigna was presently arguing that I was an assignee of the claims at issue.

Since the advent of "Who Wants to Be a Millionaire?" we perhaps feel less committed to a *final* answer until the host prompts, but if there was any doubt regarding the state of mind my opponent, the section of their reply titled "ARGUMENT" led off with "The Magistrate Judge Was Correct In Finding That Hackert Submitted Claims to Cigna As An Assignee." It would seem a stretch for even a lawyer to later equivocate and say, "It's not *our* belief that Hackert was an assignee— we were just echoing the *court's* determination that there was assignment." I offer this discourse lest it be forgotten that Cigna was at the very same time countersuing me for "enact[ing] a scheme whereby Plaintiff...continually and repeatedly misrepresented to Cigna that Plaintiff had received assignments of benefits from the Cigna Members." With Cigna endorsing the court's rejection of my declaration that I lacked assignment, how could it be a *mis*representation that I *had* assignment?

Pro pers, it seems, are up against a fixed system. Consider the words of Roderic Duncan, a former California Superior Court Judge and author of *Win Your Lawsuit: Sue in California Superior Court Without a Lawyer*. It *is*, he cautions, a "system designed by lawyers for lawyers."[15]

After another supposed *de novo* review, not surprisingly Judge Mueller found "the findings and recommendations to be supported by the record and by the proper analysis. [¶] Defendant's motion for summary judgment...is granted."

You may hear of judges "throwing out" cases when there is obviously no merit and you might imagine that Judge Mueller could not embrace the logical impossibility of me *having* assignment with respect to my suit against Cigna but *lacking* assignment for Cigna's countersuit over the very same claims. In her follow-up orders, however, Judge Mueller announced "Defendant's counterclaim remains active [¶] ... [¶] The parties shall file a joint pre-trial statement.... The final pre-trial conference is set...."

I've been called a "linear" or "black-and-white" thinker along the way, which would seem appropriate in medical practice, at least, where diagnostic workups must be decisive and algorithmic. In a computer analogy, whether I had assignment would be a state of 1 or 0, True or False, Yes or No. There simply is no "True-and-False" in Boolean logic. Yet in this legal dispute the assignment status would become more like a variable, changing at the current interest of Cigna and apparently the court itself.

PART II

Cigna v. Hackert

Chapter 15

As the court's filing deadline for the joint pretrial statement approached, Cigna's attorneys had still not extended their proposed draft for my review, whether because of disorganization, or more likely a tactic—stalling until the last minute so that I would be forced to sign off on a "joint" statement I had been given no meaningful opportunity to edit. I thus set a reasonable cut-off to receive their draft, and predictably it wasn't met. Thus resulted separate pretrial statements, neither countersigned.

Notably absent from Judge Mueller's recent orders was any invitation to file objections to her decision on the MSJ, or any discussion of recusal. Accordingly, in my version of the pretrial statement outlined according to the district court's local rules, I dedicated section "XXV. MISCELLANEOUS" to an advisement that the District Court Judge should now be disqualified per Supreme Court guidelines, writing:

> To be sure, "judicial rulings alone almost never constitute a valid basis for a bias or partiality motion." However, judicial rulings "[c]an...in the rarest circumstances evidence the degree of favoritism or antagonism required.... Almost invariably, they are proper grounds for appeal, not for recusal. [O]pinions formed by the judge on the basis of facts introduced or events occurring in the course of the current proceedings...do not constitute a basis for a bias or partiality motion *unless* they display a deep-seated favoritism or antagonism that would make fair judgment impossible." (*Liteky v. United States*, 510 U.S. 540, 114 S. Ct. 1147, 127 L. Ed. 2d 474 (1994). **Emphasis** added.)

I continued:

> As Hackert pled, the court formed "opinions" without any treatment whatsoever of key citations to caselaw

51

which were favorable to Hackert, and likewise omitted, misconstrued, or "expressly rejected" other material facts, such that the "opinions" formed were not actually based upon the pertinent facts and law. [¶] The scholarship of the Magistrate Judge and District Judge reflect their awareness...that the nonmoving party's account of the facts is to be believed; the evidence is not to be weighed.

When a jury has been requested, the ultimate fact-finding body is not the court but the jury, whose very function is to then select from among conflicting inferences and conclusions that which it considers most reasonable. See *Lopez v. Cook*, No. CIV-S-03-1605 KJM-DAD P (E.D. Cal. June 22, 2011).

I concluded:

Hackert had demanded a jury trial, but, by improperly granting Cigna's motion for summary judgment, this court divested Hackert of his constitutional *right-in-waiting* to a jury.

An "*unless*" scenario is present here, and fair judgment on Cigna's counterclaim is impossible.

In the most matter-of-fact way, plaintiff and counterdefendant presently announces to this court his intention of requesting at an appropriate time a review of this case by the Senate Judiciary Committee and/or the office of the Attorney General representing the Executive Branch according to whatever constitutional "checks and balances"...are available.

Recusal is appropriate....

Who, you might ask, determines whether a judge should be recused? The judge him- or herself of course.

As promised I did meanwhile request a separation-of-powers probe by letter to then Attorney General Jeff Sessions as well as Senator Ted Cruz, Chairman of the Senate Judiciary Committee. No, there wasn't a response, including after a resending of the letters by certified mail. There is the possibility that the post office failed to deliver the epistles to *both* recipients *twice*. Sadly the version I sent to Mr. Sessions included the comment, "[I] had the opportunity to hear your speech [on television recently] when you identified that one of your responsibilities as the Attorney General is 'to assure the fair administration of justice.'"

Fear not that I am pathetically naïve. The way I view it, this was an opportunity for our democracy to demonstrate that it is, in fact, of the people and for the people, and not, rather, of itself and for itself. "Balance of powers" is apparently just a platitude for grade school textbooks.

As for the ongoing case, I set out to make the most of the pretrial statement as the best hope of influencing, or at least preserving against, the court's all-important Final Pretrial Order.

Chapter 16

In the first section of my pretrial statement, "JURISDICTION/VENUE," I demonstrated that based on its current status the case should be dismissed, writing:

> Hackert has consistently pled and declared that he is not a[n] assignee of any Cigna beneficiary vis-à-vis ERISA. The District Court "expressly rejected" this assertion, ruling that "Cigna has carried its burden to show Hackert submitted claims as his patients' assignee...." In the context of Cigna's counterclaim at issue here, Hackert must then be considered to have assignment. Otherwise, the district court would be expressly rejecting its express rejection of Hackert's declaration that he did not have assignment, and Cigna's counterclaim must be dismissed: "'If the court determines at any time that it lacks subject-matter jurisdiction, the court must dismiss the action.' Fed. R. Civ. P. 12(h)(3)." (*SAN FRANCISCO HERRING ASSOCIATION v. US Department of Interior*, No. 15-16214 (9th Cir. Mar. 17, 2017).)
>
> "[W]here all federal claims are eliminated before trial, courts generally should decline to exercise supplemental jurisdiction over remaining state law claims." (*Ashford v. Padilla*, No. 15-17417 (9th Cir. Feb. 24, 2017).)

Under section "II. JURY/NON-JURY" I restated my election for a jury. Cigna would ultimately file two separate documents captioned "CIGNA'S PRETRIAL STATEMENT" on two different calendar days, one after the due date. At any rate, both versions stated "Hackert has requested a jury trial, to which Cigna has no objection," although they would later reconsider.

In sections "III. UNDISPUTED FACTS" and its companion "IV. DISPUTED FACTUAL ISSUES," for the sake of the record I checked every at risk factual point on a claim-by-claim and issue-by-issue basis. Facts are the currency of litigation, and the court was striving to make me legally impecunious.

In section "V. DISPUTED EVIDENTIARY ISSUES" I registered several points, and under subsection "Use of special technology at trial" requested two computer projectors and screens to impeach Cigna through side-by-side comparison of their diametric pleadings. As much as Judge Mueller seemed to disregard she clearly read this, later commenting at the pretrial conference that the infrastructure is set as-is.

For section "VI. SPECIAL FACTUAL INFORMATION IN CERTAIN ACTIONS," I illustrated once again that an oral contract would seem to have been formed by novation via my telephone call to Cigna Provider Relations, and, with respect to HMO claims, Cigna had breached a quasi-contract which "is an *obligation*...created by the law without regard to the intention of the parties." (*Unilab Corp. v. Angeles-IPA,* 244 Cal. App. 4th 622 (Cal. App. 2d Dist. 2016). Emphasis in original.) If any of the associated claims were actually *under*paid per contract or quasi-contract, they obviously could not have been *over*paid as Cigna contended.

Under the subsection "Any waiver or estoppel," I wrote:

> For the vast majority of the claims in question[,] Cigna issued, and continued to issue, Remittance Advices reporting "contractual" adjustments or referencing a "contract." Cigna formally upheld these determinations by written response to several written appeals. Cigna has to date issued no amended Remittance Advices. For the vast majority of claims in dispute, Cigna's own billing records indicate that there *was* a contract. Cigna has thereby waived its assertion that there was no contract.
>
> Hackert argues that Cigna should be estopped from repudiating an implied contract because Hackert provided the surgical assistant services with Cigna's approval ("You will be considered non-PAR." See *DEMARIA, supra.*). In Cigna's own words "Plaintiff has treated many patients whose health insurance was administered by Cigna...over [a] long period of time...."

During this period Cigna nevertheless continued to accept Hackert's services and to make payment on his claims without advising Hackert in writing that Cigna did not consider his services to be performed under an implied contract, thus inducing him to continue providing such services until this litigation revealed Cigna's posture. Any reasonable physician would have continued rendering services in that situation. Hackert would be injured if Cigna were allowed not only to break its implied contract but to take back reimbursements for work already done.

Under section "VII. RELIEF SOUGHT," the template for which did not specify anything like "For Plaintiff's/Counterclaimant's Use Only," I took the liberty to request the amounts contractually and/or quasi-contractually *under*paid; prejudgment interest; a declaration of the court; and injunctive relief of various forms if the court would deem it proper.

For section "VIII. POINTS OF LAW," the local rules requested "A statement of the legal theory or theories of recovery or of defense and of any points of law (substantive or procedural) that are or may reasonably be expected to be in controversy, citing the pertinent statutes, ordinances, regulations, cases, and other authorities relied upon." Cigna's pretrial statement blandly ran through the elements of their various causes of action, while I demonstrated the counterclaims' failure through detailed theories of defense.

In lockstep with Cigna's pleadings the district court had justified granting the motion for summary judgment partly upon the following recitation from *Wool v. Tandem Computers Inc.*, 818 F.2d 1433 (9th Cir. 1987): "[T]he dispute is genuine [when] the evidence is such that a reasonable jury could return a verdict for the nonmoving party." This, I noted, necessarily meant that no reasonable jury could *now* find that I did *not* have assignment. To parse that, the crux of the case was whether assignment of benefits existed, and, having expressly rejected my averment that I did not have assignment, the court resultingly decreed that I did. By extension, only an *un*reasonable jury could return a verdict otherwise.

There's a scene in Ayn Rand's *The Fountainhead* where the fearsome character Ellsworth Toohey argues antipodal positions back-to-back:

> In high school Ellsworth became a local celebrity—the
> star orator.... He won every debate. He could prove
> anything. Once, after beating [his opponent] with the
> affirmative of "The pen is mightier than the sword," he
> challenged [him] to reverse their positions, took the
> negative and won again.

Cigna's attorneys were likewise now reversing their stance to argue that I did *not* have assignment, and Judge Mueller appeared to abide.

In my pretrial statement I thus marshaled the legal theories of defense into contrasting sections: *"If assignment is found as a fact to be PRESENT"* and *"If assignment is found as a fact to be ABSENT."*

Here's a condensed version of what I presented under the assignment-*present* supposition.

Regarding the FIRST COUNTERCLAIM (For Recovery of Overpayment of Plan Benefits Pursuant to 29 U.S.C. § 1132(a)(3)), I argued Cigna's allegation that "Plaintiff represented to Cigna that Plaintiff had received assignments of benefits from the Cigna Members" was nugatory, that is, of no force: to the extent "Plaintiff represented to Cigna that Plaintiff had received assignments," plaintiff had assignments in fact.

Before going on to the next series of case citations, let me note that "ERISA § 502(a)(3) [is] a 'catchall provision' identical to 29 U.S.C. § 1132(a)(3)." (*Wilkins v. Baptist Healthcare System, Inc.*, 150 F.3d 609 (6th Cir. 1998).)

The American judicial system derives largely from that of England, and in a former time there were two separate courts, one of "common law" where money damages would be available, the other the "Court of Chancery" where a party could seek "equitable," that is, *non*monetary relief.

The US Supreme Court in *Montanile v. BD. OF TRUSTEES, NAT. ELEVATOR*, 136 S. Ct. 651, 577 U.S., 193 L. Ed. 2d 556 (2016) rehearsed that "[T]he term 'equitable relief' in § 502(a)(3) is limited to 'those categories of relief that were typically available in equity' during the days of the divided bench."

In the modern day "[t]he remedies of restitution and the imposition of a constructive trust are available under § 1132(a)(3), but only as true equitable remedies and provided the traditional requirements of fraud or wrong-doing are satisfied." (*CARPENTERS HEALTH AND WELFARE v. Vonderharr*, 384 F.3d 667 (9th Cir. 2004).)

"In the very same section of ERISA as § 502(a)(3), Congress authorized 'a participant or beneficiary' to bring a civil action 'to enforce his rights under the terms of the plan,' without reference to whether the relief sought is legal or equitable…. But Congress did not extend the same authorization to fiduciaries. Rather, § 502(a)(3), by its terms, only allows for equitable relief." (*Great-West Life & Annuity Ins. Co. v. Knudson*, 534 U.S. 204, 122 S. Ct. 708, 151 L. Ed. 2d 635 (2002).)

As defined by Black's, a complainant's "prayer for relief" is "A request addressed to the court and appearing at the end of the pleading; esp., a request for specific relief or damages…." Cigna's prayer, I pointed out, read "As to the *First*, Second, and Fourth Counterclaims, Cigna seeks *monetary* relief in an amount to be proved at trial." (Emphasis added.) Therefore, by its own prayer, Cigna's first counterclaim failed to state a cause of action because "monetary relief is not available under section 1132(a)(3)." (*FMC Medical Plan v. Owens*, 122 F.3d 1258 (9th Cir. 1997).)

Cigna also alleged that it "miscalculated" certain of the claims, which I argued was not the result of any wrongdoing on my part.

I further pled that Cigna disregarded ERISA's requirement to issue so-called Adverse Benefit Determinations for the asserted overpayments per 29 CFR (Code of Federal Regulations) § 2560.503-1 (m)(4)(i) and (f)(2)(iii)(B). For elaboration I cited parallels to *US RENAL CARE, INC. v. WELLSPAN HEALTH*, Civil No. 1: 14-CV-2257 (M.D. Pa. Mar. 21, 2017), an action involving "a dispute between a healthcare provider and an employee welfare benefit plan regarding alleged overpayments made to the healthcare provider…. Plaintiff brings claims pursuant to…state law and federal claims…and Defendants have responded by asserting counterclaims…. [The plan and its administrator] contend that they were not required by ERISA to send any notices of adverse benefits determinations to Plaintiff because Plaintiff was not a participant or beneficiary under the Plan. Plaintiff was, however, the assignee of a participant and beneficiary under the Plan…. Indeed, Defendants themselves argued that as [the] assignee, Plaintiff must stand in the shoes of [the patient] and cannot seek relief to which [the patient] would not be entitled as a beneficiary under the

Plan. Simply stated, Defendants cannot have it both ways. They may not contend that Plaintiff stands in [the] shoes in order to limit Plaintiff's potential remedies, but then argue that Plaintiff is not entitled to notices of adverse benefits determinations as [the] assignee."

I also argued that Cigna failed to "prove up" through reference to specific claims and plan documents how I had "wrongfully obtained" payments.

The SECOND COUNTERCLAIM for Unjust Enrichment, I wrote, is a state-law cause of action, as evidenced by Cigna's own citation to California, not federal, caselaw, *Lectrodryer v. SeoulBank*, 91 Cal. Rptr. 2d 881, 77 Cal. App. 4th 723, 77 Cal. 4th 723 (Ct. App. 2000). In the context of assignment being present, Cigna's state law causes of action are federally preempted: "[A]ny state-law cause of action that duplicates, supplements, or supplants the ERISA civil enforcement remedy conflicts with the clear congressional intent to make the ERISA remedy exclusive and is therefore pre-empted. The pre-emptive force of ERISA § 502(a) is still stronger." (*Davila, supra*.) "[T]he Ninth Circuit has expressly refused to create *federal* common law causes of action under ERISA." (*CHERENE v. FIRST AMERICAN FINANCIAL CORPORATION LONG-TERM DISABILITY PLAN*, No. C 03-02226 MJJ (N.D. Cal. Feb. 17, 2004). Emphasis added.)

Notwithstanding federal preemption, Cigna also failed to establish the essential element that I *unjustly* retained payments at the expense of Cigna, because, I pled, there was no wrongdoing on my part, and Cigna had not proved its assertion that any claims were *over*paid.

Lastly, Cigna's "Prayer for Relief" read, again, "[a]s to the First, *Second*, and Fourth Counterclaims, Cigna seeks *monetary* relief in an amount to be proved at trial," yet "[u]just enrichment is an equitable rather than a legal claim." (*McKesson HBOC v. NEW YORK STATE COMMON RETIREMENT*, 339 F.3d 1087 (9th Cir. 2003).) "[P]laintiffs may not disguise an attempt to obtain monetary relief as a traditional equitable remedy." (*Gabriel v. Alaska Elec. Pension Fund*, 773 F.3d 945 (9th Cir. 2014).)

Regarding the THIRD COUNTERCLAIM (Constructive Trust), I described as conclusory Cigna's allegation that "Plaintiff obtained payments for health care services in amounts exceeding the amounts

Cigna was obligated to pay Plaintiff" and that "Plaintiff is the constructive trustee of those amounts, for the benefit of Cigna." As per the *Owens* court, "a constructive trust is born from some form of *ill*-gotten gain of another's property" (emphasis added), but just as "Owens did not gain FMC's medical payments by any form of fraud, duress, or unconscionable behavior," neither did I from Cigna, I pled.

But even presuming *arguendo* ("for the sake of argument" in Latin) that my gains *were* ill-gotten, I contended that Cigna could only "seek restitution...in the form of a constructive trust...where money...could clearly be traced to particular funds or property in the defendant's possession.... But where the property [sought to be recovered] or its proceeds have been dissipated so that no product remains...the plaintiff cannot enforce a constructive trust of...*other* property of the [defendant]." (*Great-West, supra.* Emphasis added.)

I quoted the Ninth Circuit in *Honolulu Joint Local Union No. 675 v. Foster*, 332 F.3d 1234 (9th Cir. 2003): "The Supreme Court cases interpreting § 1132(a)(3) mark a steadily shrinking field of appropriate equitable relief available to plan fiduciaries," and "only in limited circumstances, where there is an identifiable *res*"—a Latin word here representing the "property sought to be recovered." The Supreme Court in *Montanile* held that "when [a party] dissipates the whole [*res*] on nontraceable items, the fiduciary cannot bring a suit to attach the [party's] general assets under § 502(a)(3)." Cigna alleged overpayment of $2,980.41 under this family of counterclaims but failed to trace the figure to particular funds in my possession, and, I argued, this relatively meager *res* was dissipated over the course of the several years gone by so that no product remains.

I noted that the FOURTH COUNTERCLAIM (Common Count — Money Had and Received) is a state law action (see, e.g., *US CAPITAL PARTNERS, LLC v. AHMSA INTERNATIONAL, INC.*, No. 12-6520 JSC (N.D. Cal. Feb. 14, 2013), and would thus be federally preempted per *Davila*. Notwithstanding, "To prevail on a claim for money due and owing (also referred to as money had and received) Plaintiff must show unjust enrichment of the wrongdoer, and in order for plaintiff to recover in such action she must show that a definite sum, to which she is justly entitled, has been received by defendant." (*AHMSA, supra.*) Cigna, I pled, had not proved up a definite sum but merely tallied a series of dollar amounts in a table in its counterclaim, and had also not shown *just* entitlement. While Cigna alleged the payments "greatly exceeded" their obligation, "to not consider the terms of the plan...would be to accept the insurer's overpayment determination at face value." (*PREMIER HEALTH CENTER, PC v. UNITEDHEALTH GROUP*, Civ. No. 11-425 (ES) (D.N.Y. Aug. 1, 2013).)

Cigna not only failed to establish the elements of its fourth counterclaim but, by alleging a common count, relinquished its more foreboding group of allegations, the so-called torts. Black's defines a tort as "a civil wrong, other than breach of contract, for which a remedy may be obtained, usu. in the form of damages...." Black's provides this definition for a common count: "In a plaintiff's pleading in an action for debt, boilerplate language that is not founded on the circumstances of the individual case but is intended to guard against a possible variance and to enable the plaintiff to take advantage of any ground of liability that the proof may disclose. In the action for indebitatus assumpsit, the common count stated that the defendant had failed to pay a debt as promised." Black's defines "indebitatus assumpsit," in turn, simply as "being indebted." In the words of the California Court of Appeal, "since the basic premise for pleading a common count in a situation as presented here is that the person is thereby 'waiving the tort and suing in assumpsit,' any tort damages are out." (*Zumbrun v. University of Southern California*, 25 Cal. App. 3d 1, 101 Cal. Rptr. 499 (Ct. App. 1972).)

Somewhat like a geometry proof where the student puts to paper even the most obvious, I noted that "fraud is a tort," citing the Supreme Court in *National Bank & Loan Co. v. Petrie*, 189 U.S. 423, 23 S. Ct. 512, 47 L. Ed. 879 (1903). Per the *Zumbrun* analysis, I argued, Cigna waived both its Fifth Counterclaim for Fraud and Sixth for Negligent Misrepresentation, which is likewise a tort. (*Bily v. Arthur Young & Co.*, 834 P.2d 745, 3 Cal. 4th 370, 11 Cal. Rptr. 2d 51 (1992).)

But on the perilous fraud allegations I was not about to surrender any legal rights by stopping there. The long-range view was an appeal to the Ninth Circuit and I would not want to seem even slightly complacent. In law probably the only absolute is "never say never." I thus marched on regarding the FIFTH COUNTERCLAIM (Fraud). Once again I invoked federal preemption of this state-law cause of action per *Davila*. Pointing to the utter lack of particularity and specificity, I highlighted Cigna's departure from the preceding individual counterclaims which had reincorporated the "FACTUAL ALLEGATIONS" appearing early in its counterclaim-at-large, but by reference were specifically omitted from the fraud-based counterclaims, without substitute. Per *Kearns v. Ford Motor Co.*, 567 F.3d 1120 (9th Cir. 2009) which Cigna itself would cite for the elements, "state claims are subject to Rule 9(b) of the Federal Rules of Civil Procedure...which requires that allegations of fraud be pleaded with particularity.... Because we find that Kearns's claims were all grounded in fraud, his failure to plead the [complaint] with particularity merited its dismissal."

Moving on to further examination I iterated the elements: (1) a misrepresentation, false representation, concealment, or nondisclosure; (2) knowledge of falsity, or scienter (from Latin "to know"—think of the English word "science"); (3) intent to defraud or to induce reliance; (4) justifiable reliance; and (5) resulting damage.

In this section of my pretrial statement where assignment was presumed *present*, it would have seemed merely for good measure to point out that Cigna's fraud allegations were nullified by the essential element, *mis*representation: to the extent plaintiff represented to Cigna that plaintiff had received assignment, plaintiff had assignment in fact; therefore, what plaintiff "represented" to Cigna—that he had received assignments—could not reasonably be considered a "misrepresentation, false representation, concealment, or nondisclosure."

For thoroughness, and in part to foreshadow the discussion to follow in the assignment-*absent* section, I addressed the remaining elements as well.

As to knowledge of falsity, scienter, I wrote that if the alleged representation is true, it does not follow that the representor could have knowledge of its falsity. But, I continued, if the court should further entertain Cigna's fraud allegations, with respect to any "representation" my knowledge was that I had followed a well-established industry standard to submit claims on behalf of patients, which is provided for even in the plan documents: "Out-of-Network claims can be submitted by the provider if the provider is able and willing to file on your behalf." I also brought to the court's attention the following caveat found within plan documents: "Medical Benefits are assignable to the provider.... [¶ but] Cigna may, at its option, make

63

payment to you for the cost of any Covered Expenses from a Non-Participating Provider *even if benefits have been assigned.*" (Emphasis added.) If Cigna reserved the right to issue payment to the member rather than the provider even if assigned, and out-of-network claims *can* be submitted by the provider on a member's behalf, it would seem even more apparent that claims were being submitted as a courtesy to the patients.

As to intent to defraud or to induce reliance, I wrote Cigna cannot reasonably allege that it was "fraudulently induced" to remit payment to a provider designated by Cigna itself as "non-PAR" when per the plan documents Cigna administers it reserved the right to issue benefits to the member with or without assignment.

As to justifiable reliance, I wrote, the counterclaim suggests that "payors such as Cigna rely on the accuracy and truthfulness of the claims submissions in adjudicating the claims," but does not plead with specificity and particularity how any of my claims were materially inaccurate or untruthful, and, even if they were, why Cigna would have *justifiably* relied upon them to its detriment. A healthcare services corporation of Cigna's stature would presumably be knowledgeable of industry standards such as the expectation that providers will submit claims on behalf of patients when at all possible, and should also be aware of the language in the plan documents it is administering.

As to resulting damage, I wrote, even if all other elements of fraud were met, Cigna made the unqualified assertion that it was "damaged by Plaintiff's misrepresentations *because* Cigna made payments to Plaintiff...in reliance upon Plaintiff's misrepresentations." Even if Cigna did make these unsubstantiated payments to me, its outlay would seem to reflect precisely the same amount it would have disbursed to its members instead of the provider. Cigna supplied no evidence that it might have adjudicated a different *level* of payment had it remitted the benefits to its members rather than me. "No damages, no case" is a tenet in law.

Negligent Misrepresentation, the SIXTH COUNTERCLAIM, differs from Fraud only with respect to the second element where the alleged misrepresentation is made "*without reasonable grounds* for believing it to be true." (See, e.g., *Apollo Capital Fund, LLC v. Roth Capital Partners, LLC*, 70 Cal. Rptr. 3d 199, 158 Cal. App. 4th 226 (Ct. App.

2007).) Nugatory in the assignment-present context.

Regarding the SEVENTH COUNTERCLAIM (Unfair Competition in Violation of Business and Professions Code §§ 17200, et seq.), the pseudo-elements may be found in the case Cigna would cite, *Farmers Ins. Exchange v. Superior Court*, 2 Cal.4th 377, 383 (1992), as a proscription against "'unlawful, unfair, or fraudulent' business practices....[which] 'borrows violations of other laws and treats them as unlawful practices that the unfair competition law makes independently actionable.'"

I argued once again that with assignment present, this state-law claim was not only federally preempted by *Davila* but inoperative. Cigna's pleading that "Plaintiff enacted a scheme whereby Plaintiff submitted claims to Cigna...and continually and repeatedly misrepresented to Cigna that Plaintiff had received assignments of benefits from the Cigna Members" would be no misrepresentation at all, and thus plaintiff did not "fraudulently induce[] Cigna to pay claims that it is otherwise not responsible for paying."

All of that was of course the "easy" part. The real challenge would be confronting the shape-shifters looming about. Thankfully I was well prepared by some great instructors along the way, like Mr. George Krohn in middle school social studies who put a character up on the blackboard one day, identified by the class when asked as the letter "X." In mock reprimand he said, "No!...that's my signature!" He then erased the figure and redrew another that looked virtually identical to the first, and asked again: "What's *this*?" The class dutifully responded, "Your signature....," but he shook his head and said "No, that's an 'X.'" This was of course an exercise in power and corruption, and the application here is that Cigna's ilk of lawyers will say anything, and the court had the prerogative to favor whatever side it pleased.

Accepting the mutability of a "material fact," what follows in the next chapter is a synopsis of the legal theories of defense I presented in my pretrial statement under the assignment-*absent* scenario.

Chapter 17

I opened the section "If assignment is found as a fact to be ABSENT" with a look back: "Preliminarily, any of the legal theories of defense and any of the points of law presented in the preceding section titled 'If assignment is found as a fact to be PRESENT' which have independent application to this section...are hereby incorporated as if fully set forth herein, and are not waived."

I then quoted a similar case, *CONNECTICUT GENERAL LIFE INSURANCE COMPANY v. LA PEER SURGERY CENTER LLC*, No. 2: 13-cv-03726-CAS (JCGx) (C.D. Cal. Mar. 12, 2014): "[B]ecause the [complaint] does not disclose the identity of the ERISA plans, those plans are effectively proceeding as anonymous plaintiffs. Allowing plaintiffs to proceed anonymously, however, is disfavored because it runs afoul of the public's common law right of access to judicial proceedings. As such, because [i]t is the responsibility of the complainant clearly to allege facts demonstrating that [it] is a proper party to invoke judicial resolution of the dispute and the exercise of the court's remedial powers...the Court concludes that the complaint must be dismissed."

I next distinguished the difference between assignment *of* benefits and the benefits themselves for a given claim, explaining that benefits are not a function of assignment. That is to say, reimbursement is computed without consideration of whether the provider has assignment. No plan documents suggested that the benefits payable are determined by the *assignment* status. Cigna, I argued, failed to show how any alleged wrongdoing on my part affected the reimbursement *level* Cigna adjudicated. Any "mistake" with respect to, for example, *network* status, was completely Cigna's own considering my repeated efforts to elucidate how Cigna was processing these claims.

I revisited how Cigna's entire counterclaim revolved around such keyword allegations as "wrongdoing," "unjust," "ill-gotten," or "fraud," but that caselaw regarding the construct of assignment is varied and conflicting. Whereas in other circuits assignment must be in writing, in the Ninth per *Misic*, it need only be "*valid.*"

I explored the tangent of *scope* of assignment via the case *IN RE WELLPOINT, INC. OUT-OF-NETWORK "UCR" RATE*, 903 F. Supp. 2d 880 (C.D. Cal. 2012)[16]: "[T]he Ninth Circuit has recently reiterated that courts must look to the language of an ERISA assignment itself to determine the scope of the assigned claims. [¶] The Court's task in interpreting the scope of an assignment is to enforce the intent of the parties. In determining what rights or interest pass under an assignment, the intention of the parties as manifested in the instrument is controlling."

But, I asked, what was the intent of the parties if there was no written instrument? I turned once again to *Klay*:

> When a patient receives care from an out-of-network physician, the physician can attempt to receive payment directly from the [plan] as a courtesy to the patient or the physician can receive a direct assignment of the patient's contractual right to reimbursement from the [plan]. Because the treating physician does not participate in the patient's plan, such claims for reimbursement are referred to as "non-par" claims.

Klay was exculpatory, I argued. Having been designated by Cigna as non-PAR, although I may not have had "direct" assignment, claims were submitted to Cigna as a *courtesy* to the members, non-fraudulently.

The declaration that I was not an assignee vis-à-vis ERISA was consistent with the above model, I pled, because per decisions like *Connecticut State Dental v. Anthem Health Plans*, 591 F.3d 1337 (11th Cir. 2009), "it is well-established in this and most other circuits that a healthcare provider may acquire derivative standing...under ERISA by obtaining a *written* assignment from a participant or beneficiary of his right to payment of medical benefits." (Emphasis added.)

Next I touched on the concept of *anti*-assignment. Cigna was alleging overpayments on the basis that I misrepresented assignment, yet, as I meticulously cataloged in the DISPUTED FACTUAL ISSUES section of the pretrial statement, several of the plan documents contained an anti-assignment clause, reading, for example: "Medical Benefits are not assignable...." The Ninth Circuit had established that

"Anti-assignment clauses in ERISA plans are valid and enforceable." (*SPINEDEX, supra.*) For most of the other claims the plan documents stated "Cigna may, at its option, make payment to you for the cost of any Covered Expenses from a Non-Participating Provider *even if benefits have been assigned.*" (Emphasis added.) For a couple other claims the plans read "Definitions of terms we use in this brochure: [¶] Assignment: Your authorization for us to pay benefits directly to the provider. We reserve the right to pay you directly for all covered services." For another claim the plan documents stated: "Assignment of Benefits [¶] Benefits will be paid directly to the hospital or the individual performing the service unless the provider of services indicates on the claim form that payment has been received directly from the patient...." This plan seemed to call for payment to the provider with or without assignment, the only exception being if the patient had already been billed.

Since the plans in question generally either did not allow assignment or gave Cigna discretion to remit payment to the member rather than the provider even when there may have been assignment, I argued Cigna could not reasonably prosecute me on the basis that it was fraudulently induced to issue payments to me.

Worms have many hearts and that's why we're told as children not to be overly concerned if these creatures may become wounded: as long as there's a heart, the worm will live. By corollary, if I envisioned my adversary a "worm" of sorts, perhaps it would not be prudent to consider their *case* dead without a full complement of fatal strikes, and so I went on to specifically address each of the individual counterclaims in the assignment-*absent* scenario.

Regarding the FIRST COUNTERCLAIM (For Recovery of Overpayment of Plan Benefits Pursuant to 29 U.S.C. § 1132(a)(3)), I argued the counterclaim fails as a matter of law because there is no federal jurisdiction in the absence of assignment, and there is by definition no *state*-law cause of action for the federally encoded "Recovery of Overpayment under 29 U.S.C. § 1132(a)(3)."

Notwithstanding, if the tribunal should find that Cigna could seek to recover alleged overpayments pursuant to § 1132(a)(3), Cigna had still failed to properly plead any wrongdoing on my part by the clear & convincing standard.

As to the SECOND COUNTERCLAIM (Unjust Enrichment), I

referenced the earlier arguments and also made note that "unjust enrichment" was one of my own *affirmative defenses*—described in Chapter 18. Considering the facts and circumstances as a whole, it would be unjust for Cigna to prevail.

Concerning the THIRD COUNTERCLAIM (Constructive Trust), I cited another passage from *Zumbrun*: "It is hornbook law that the purpose of a complaint is to furnish the defendants with certain definite charges which can be intelligently met....The point is that the accuser must place his finger squarely and directly upon whatever dereliction is relied upon."

The phrase "hornbook law" seems to date back to the sixteenth century when English monks made "hornbooks" to help pupils learn to read, usually in the form of a wooden paddle with an alphabet and a verse, deriving their name from the piece of transparent horn protecting the surface.[17] Per Black's, the term "hornbook" in law conveys that the subject matter is "old, fundamental, and well settled," and thus rudimentary.

Here, Cigna neglected to place its finger directly upon the asserted dereliction by failing to identify and trace the constructive trust it claimed.

Cigna would reference *Burlesci v. Petersen*, 80 Cal. Rptr. 2d 704, 68 Cal. App. 4th 1062, 68 Cal. 4th 1062 (Ct. App. 1998) for the elements, although actually an unsupportive case: "A constructive trust is an involuntary equitable trust created by operation of law as a remedy to compel the transfer of property from the person wrongfully holding it to the rightful owner. The essence of the theory of constructive trust is to...prevent a person from taking advantage of...wrongdoing [or] mistake...unless he or she has some other and better right thereto. [A] constructive trust may only be imposed where the following three conditions are satisfied: (1) the existence of a res (property or some interest in property); (2) the right of a complaining party to that res; and (3) some wrongful acquisition or detention of the res by another party who is not entitled to it."

I pled that I had already demonstrated "some other and better right" than Cigna through quantum meruit. If there was any question regarding which party was equitably entitled to said *res*, it would seem I because a payer of Cigna's stature knows, or should know, that assistant surgeons submit claims on behalf of patients according to industry standards, and moreover it was I who had requested but was denied an audit of the claims. Finally, no matter what party might be the equitable holder of the proposed *res*, as of that point in time it was no longer even in existence—a required element—as those modest funds were long dissipated.

Regarding the FOURTH COUNTERCLAIM (Common Count – Money Had and Received), I argued that even in the absence of assignment, the preceding points and authorities served to demonstrate a failure to state this claim. Cigna had not actually proved up a "definite sum" as this cause requires.

As to the FIFTH COUNTERCLAIM (Fraud) and SIXTH (Negligent Misrepresentation), notwithstanding Cigna's waiver of these torts by suing in the assumpsit (*Zumbrun*), I reemphasized that the counterclaims' absolute lack of particularity and specificity failed to meet the necessary clear & convincing standard.

For the SEVENTH COUNTERCLAIM (Unfair Competition in Violation of Business and Professions Code §§ 17200, et seq.), I argued that, if I were found not to have assignment, Cigna could not avoid the anti-assignment language within the plan documents. Accordingly, there was no role for the injunctive relief requested under the counterclaim. Cigna would otherwise be enjoined from following the terms of its own plans.

I commented that a *declaration*, however, would seem welcome by both parties to clarify what their respective rights and responsibil-ities finally were moving forward. Unlike Bill Murray's *Groundhog Day* which culminates in a happy ending, I for one had no interest in reliving this scene.

Chapter 18

The next subsection of my pretrial statement under "VIII. POINTS OF LAW" was dedicated to the *affirmative* defenses. In contrast to the preceding theories which would generally be classified as *negative* defenses (a *denial* of the allegations), affirmative defenses are defined by Black's Law Dictionary as "A defendant's assertion of facts and arguments that, if true, will defeat the plaintiff's...claim, even if all the allegations in the complaint are true...." Black's points to the insanity plea as one example in a criminal case. Having enumerated my affirmative defenses in the answer to the counterclaim per Fed. Rule Civ. Proc. 8(c), I further developed them as follows.

Estoppel

The elements of equitable estoppel are "(1) conduct by which one induces another to believe in certain material facts; and (2) the inducement results in acts in justifiable reliance thereon; and (3) the resulting acts cause injury." (*Button v. Connecticut General Life Ins. Co.*, 847 F.2d 584 (9th Cir. 1988).) "A plan administrator may not fail to give a reason for a benefits denial during the administrative process and then raise that reason for the first time when the denial is challenged in federal court...." (*Harlick v. Blue Shield of California*, 686 F.3d 699 (9th Cir. 2012).) I argued that Cigna's counterclaim was retaliatory, as evidenced by the fact that it was now repudiating how it adjudicated over thirty claims "per your Cigna fee schedule according to your contract." By concealing its apparent position, Cigna had induced me to continue offering surgical assistant services to their members. The pleadings to date, I argued, demonstrated that any mistake was at Cigna's hands, and it would be injurious for Cigna to be allowed to "claw back" those reimbursements.

Failure to Mitigate

"The reasonableness of a [party's] efforts to mitigate is a question of fact for jury determination." (*Jackson v. Shell Oil Co.*, 702 F.2d 197 (9th Cir. 1983).) Considering that I had repeatedly and ever more formally asked Cigna to clarify how it was adjudicating claims before ultimately invoking litigation and inciting this counterlitigation, it was clear, I argued, that Cigna failed to mitigate any damages, restitution, or other relief it now sought.

Set-Off

For this affirmative defense I cited a Mueller decision: "[T]he equitable right of offset reduces a defendant's liability by the amount of any mutual debt between the two, thus avoiding the absurdity of making A pay B when B owes A. [A] court of equity will compel a set-off when mutual demands are held under such circumstances that one of them should be applied against the other and only the balance recovered." (*FDIC v. Ching*, 189 F. Supp. 3d 978 (E.D. Cal. 2016). "Without an offset, plaintiffs will receive an improper windfall." (*Corder v. Brown*, 25 F.3d 833 (9th Cir. 1994).) There were, I argued, several claims among those at issue which were objectively *under*paid:

- A bariatric HMO claim subject to quasi-contractual reimbursement at "reasonable and customary value"
- The MultiPlan silent PPO claims for which California Insurance Code requires written disclosure while Cigna attested there was no written contract
- At least one "zero pay" claim where the associated plan documents stated "Cigna will consider claims for coverage...when...a claim...is submitted...for Out-of-Network benefits after services are rendered," and the benefits "Schedule" reads: "Assistant Surgeon [¶] The maximum amount payable will be limited to charges made by an assistant surgeon that do not exceed a percentage of the surgeon's allowable charge as specified in Cigna Reimbursement Policies"

Unclean hands

"Under this doctrine, plaintiffs seeking equitable relief must have acted fairly and without fraud or deceit as to the controversy in issue. [¶] ... [¶] In California, the unclean hands doctrine applies not only to equitable claims, but also to legal ones. The court examine[s]...the nature of the misconduct at issue and the misconduct's equitable impact on the relationship between the parties and the injuries claimed." (*Adler v. Federal Republic of Nigeria*, 219 F.3d 869 (9th Cir. 2000).) I argued that Cigna should be barred from the relief it sought by the doctrine of unclean hands because it had not acted fairly, as I pled throughout. Cigna had not been asleep to some artifice I had "schemed to enact," just now realizing I was "overpaid" and must be "disgorged" of "ill-gotten gains." Cigna, I remarked, may wish to project an image of being a healthcare benefactor when in reality it is first and foremost a business, and as such seeks to maximize profits above all else. The present counterclaim is evidence, I proposed, that Cigna will resort to meritless litigation to intimidate providers it may consider unruly.

Waiver

With a separate discussion of the Statute of Limitations to follow, I noted California courts have found that "A statute of limitations issue is a waiver issue." (*Kennedy, Cabot & Co. v. NATL. ASSN. OF SEC.*, 41 Cal. App. 4th 1167, 49 Cal. Rptr. 2d 66 (Ct. App. 1996).) I also reiterated that Cigna waived any opportunity to recover the asserted overpayments by failing to timely and properly issue Adverse Benefit Determinations.

Statute of Limitations

"Congress not infrequently fails to supply an express statute of limitations when it creates a federal cause of action. When that occurs, [w]e have generally concluded that Congress intended that the courts apply the most closely analogous statute of limitations under state law." (*Reed v. Transportation Union*, 488 U.S. 319, 109 S. Ct. 621, 102 L. Ed. 2d 665 (1989).) "Because the civil enforcement section of ERISA, § 502, 29 U.S.C. § 1132, does not provide its own statute of limitations, courts must determine the applicable limitation period." (*Felton v. Unisource Corp.*, 940 F.2d 503 (9th Cir. 1991).) "When determining the correct limitation statute, we are bound by the Supreme Court's admonition that analogous state statutes of limitations are to be used unless they frustrate or significantly interfere with federal policies." (*Id.*) "Therefore, we must look to [the forum state's] law for the most analogous statute of limitations." (*Id.*) "The first step towards determining what limitations period should apply is to characterize the federal claim in state law terms." (*Id.*) "We must determine the essence of the federal statutory claim to guide our selection of an analogous state law cause of action." (*Id.*)

I pled that the most analogous state law claim for recovery of an alleged overpayment would be California Insurance Code § 10133.66(b): "Reimbursement requests for the overpayment of a claim shall not be made...unless a written request for reimbursement is sent to the provider within 365 days of the date of payment on the overpaid claim. The written notice shall...include a clear explanation of the basis upon which it is believed the amount paid on the claim was in excess of the amount due.... The 365-day time limit shall not apply if the overpayment was caused in whole or in part by fraud or misrepresentation on the part of the provider." I recognized that Cigna would object that the alleged overpayments *were* caused by fraud, but the regulation does not say, for example, mere "*allegations* of fraud," and so proposed to the court, would a provider demand a comprehensive claims audit, as I did, if it was simultaneously setting out to defraud the payer?

"A [statute of limitations] claim ordinarily accrues when [a] plaintiff has a complete and present cause of action." (*Petrella v. Metro-Goldwyn-Mayer, Inc.*, 134 S. Ct. 1962, 188 L. Ed. 2d 979, 572 U.S. (2014).) However, "while a statute of limitations normally sets the time within which proceedings must be commenced once a cause of action accrues, the statute of repose limits the time within which an action may be brought and is not related to accrual. Indeed, the injury need not have occurred, much less have been discovered. Unlike an ordinary statute of limitations which begins running upon accrual of the claim, [the] period contained in a statute of repose begins when a specific event occurs..... A statute of repose thus is harsher than a statute of limitations in that it cuts off a right of action after a specified period of time, irrespective of accrual or even notice that a legal right has been invaded." (*Giest v. Sequoia Ventures, Inc.*, 99 Cal. Rptr. 2d 476, 83 Cal. App. 4th 300 (Ct. App. 2000).) California Insurance Code § 10133.66(b) is by inspection a statute of repose, I noted, and Cigna did not invoke any request for a refund of asserted overpayments within 365 days from the date of payment. I argued that Cigna's action for alleged claim overpayments was therefore time barred.

Total Performance

My understanding of the affirmative defense of "total" or "full performance" is that if a party has met its obligations, it cannot be considered liable for other associated claims against it. Examination of the spreadsheet prepared by Cigna showed that most claims were adjudicated as under contract, and remained so after my several appeals. Cigna had not pled any form of breach of contract against me, and there was no evidence of incomplete performance of the terms of the apparent contract Cigna had referenced in its remittance advices or responses to the appeal letters. "Extracontractual, compensatory and punitive damages are not available under ERISA." (*Bast v. Prudential Ins. Co. of America*, 150 F.3d 1003 (9th Cir. 1998).) Therefore, I argued, Cigna's effort to retract payments in the improper guise of ERISA regulations must be considered "extracontractual" and thus barred.

No Statutory Violations

In the absence of any statutory violations by me, I argued Cigna's counterclaim for return of overpayments was barred to any extent the demands relied on such violations.

Unjust Enrichment

I quoted back to Judge Mueller her *FDIC v. Ching* decision once more: "Unjust enrichment is a separate general principle underlying various legal doctrines and remedies. Stated simply, it allows the recovery of a benefit unjustly retained. A critical limitation on this rule is that one who confers a benefit officiously is not entitled to restitution." I brought into focus how Cigna placed itself into a quandary. "Fraud is a serious allegation." (*US EX REL. SCHARFF v. CAMELOT COUNSELING*, No. 13-cv-3791 (PKC) (S.D.N.Y. Sept. 28, 2016).[18] Cigna's counterclaim alleged that "Plaintiff made fraudulent misrepresentations on claims submissions to Cigna, when he claimed he had received assignments of benefits from Cigna Members." Yet Cigna had earlier pled that "Plaintiff must be proceeding as an assignee," "The Magistrate Judge Was Correct In Finding That Hackert Submitted Claims to Cigna As An Assignee." It could not be considered just for a party to plead the same fact as both true and false at different times according to its present interests.

Chapter 19

Most of the remaining sections of my pretrial statement were fairly routine—witness list, exhibits, discovery documents, anticipated pretrial motions, etc. Having every expectation, however, that Judge Mueller was going to railroad the upcoming trial in Cigna's favor, I did confront the specter of attorney fees in its section, XXII. Cigna was seeking about $2,900 for the non-fraud counterclaims and roughly ten times that for the fraud based allegations, but what was really at stake was the payroll of the lawyers, in excess of $250,000 I would imagine.

The counterclaim had requested attorney fees pursuant to California Civil Procedure Code section 1021.5 on the basis that "the relief sought herein, if granted, will vindicate important rights affecting the public interest, including, but not limited to, California's proscriptions against fraudulent billing." I pointed out that the counterclaim itself stated "[t]he disputed claims at issue in this litigation [are] all...governed by...ERISA." Cigna characterized its countersuit as wholly federal, yet was seeking attorney fees under a state provision, so, even if it were to prevail, I suggested the fees requested under California law should not be available.

Presuming the court would ignore the inconsistency, I referenced *Honolulu Joint Local Union* where the Ninth Circuit expounded on ERISA's hurdles against attorney fees: "ERISA, 29 U.S.C. § 1132(g)...provides that '[i]n any action under this subchapter ... by a participant, beneficiary, or fiduciary, the court in its discretion may allow a reasonable attorney's fee and costs of action to either party.' There are five factors that govern the decision to award or deny attorney's fees: (1) the degree of the opposing party's culpability or bad faith, (2) the ability of the opposing party to satisfy an award of fees, (3) whether an award of fees against the opposing party would deter others from acting in similar circumstances, (4) whether the party requesting fees sought to benefit all participants and beneficiaries of an ERISA plan or to resolve a significant legal question regarding ERISA, and (5) the relative merits of the parties' positions."

Even if Judge Mueller might greenlight Cigna's petition for attorney fees, perhaps the Ninth Circuit would temper the insult by that formula.

Chapter 20

I lost even more confidence in the court when at the pretrial conference Judge Mueller kept calling me "*Mr.* Hackert," not "Dr."

Titles themselves mean very little to me, and in Commonwealth countries, surgeons, in contrast to other physicians, *are* typically addressed as "mister" instead of "doctor." But it wasn't my impression that Judge Mueller is some type of Anglophile. Rather, I feared she simply wasn't paying that much attention to the case, or disdained at least one of its parties.

As to the substance of the conference, in what I would've expected to be no more than a walk-through of the pretrial statement material, when Judge Mueller asked the parties to confirm that it would not be a bench but a jury trial, through attorney Jennifer Nguyen, Cigna for the first time objected to my jury demand.

The judge could and surely should have said something along the lines of "The time to contest a jury trial has passed with the filing of the pretrial statements." She resolved, instead, that each side should file a brief regarding the role for a jury on Cigna's counterclaim.

And no, Judge Mueller advised, there would be no self-disqualification.

Chapter 21

Although the right to a jury would appear at first to be "inviolate," there are exceptions to everything. My brief regarding the role for a jury acknowledged head on the judicial discretion potentially imparted by Fed. R. Civ. P. 39(a) reading, "When a jury trial has been demanded under Rule 38, the action must be designated on the docket as a jury action. The trial on all issues so demanded must be by jury *unless*[¶] the court, on motion or on its own, finds that on some or all of those issues there is no federal right to a jury trial." (Emphasis added.)

So, what were the federal rights to a jury in this case?

My adversary's evaluation was captioned "CIGNA'S BRIEF RE: NO RIGHT TO JURY TRIAL ON EQUITABLE CLAIMS," which first recapped that "Cigna asserts the following counterclaims against Hackert: (1) recovery of overpayment of benefits pursuant to 29 U.S.C. §1132(a)(3); (2) unjust enrichment; (3) constructive trust; (4) money had and received; (5) fraud; (6) negligent misrepresentation; and (7) unfair competition in violation of Business and Professions Code § 17200 et seq."

Should there have been any prior confusion regarding the direction of their allegations, the brief explained that "If Hackert received assignments of benefits from the Cigna members...Cigna asserts the first, second, third, and fourth counterclaims against Hackert," but argued that "[b]ecause Cigna seeks only equitable relief in its first, second, third, fourth, and seventh counterclaims, Hackert is not entitled to a jury trial on those claims."

By citation to *Chauffeurs, Teamsters and Helpers Local No. 391 v. Terry*, 494 U.S. 588, 565 (1990) Cigna conceded that "the right to a jury trial exists...where legal rights are at issue," accepting that "the counterclaims for fraud and negligent misrepresentation are issues of fact that may be appropriately determined by a jury[¶]...if Hackert did not receive assignments of benefits...."

Cigna's brief avoided the question of just who would determine the assignment status, but I made sure to stress in mine that "the presence, validity, scope, and context of assignment [is] a material issue to be found by the demanded jury as the trier of fact."

To the heart of their brief, Cigna argued "there is no right to jury trial for claims brought under, or preempted by, section 502 of ERISA. *See, Thomas v. Oregon Fruit Products Co.*, 228 F.3d. 991, 996 (9th Cir. 2000)." My brief also cited *Oregon Fruit Products* by which I provisionally ceded "there is no '*independent* constitutional or statutory right to jury trial in ERISA actions'" (emphasis added), but I would go on to illustrate the *dependent* function of a jury with respect to even the equitable issues.

Lawyers certainly have a duty to vigorously represent their clients, but only to the ethical limits set by such authorities as the ABA, the American Bar Association, which promulgates in its *Model Rules of Professional Conduct* that "A lawyer shall not knowingly [¶] fail to disclose to the tribunal legal authority in the controlling jurisdiction known to the lawyer to be directly adverse to the position of the client...."[19]

Counter to such guidelines, Cigna's brief included the following isolated quotation from the Ninth Circuit's *Teutscher v. Woodson*, 835 F.3d 936, 943 (9th Cir. 2016): "It is well settled that there is no right to a jury trial where 'equitable rights alone [are] recognized, and equitable remedies [are] administered.'"

As it turned out I would cite this very same *Teutscher* case in my corresponding brief, though not in the fashion of a sound bite but capturing the opinion as a whole:

> The Supreme Court has explained how to comport with the Seventh Amendment when trying legal and equitable claims in the same action. In *Dairy Queen, Inc. v. Wood*, 369 U.S. 469, 82 S.Ct. 894, 8 L.Ed.2d 44 (1962), the Court held that in cases in which legal and equitable claims turn on common issues of fact, any legal issues for which a trial by jury is timely and properly demanded [must] be submitted to a jury, and the jury's determination of the legal claims must occur prior to any final court determination of [the] equitable claims[.] [B]ecause the Seventh Amendment's second clause prohibit[s] ... the courts of the United States to re-examine any facts tried by a jury except as permitted

under the narrow modes known to the common law, the court then must abide by the jury's findings of fact in making any subsequent rulings. [I]t would be a violation of the seventh amendment right to jury trial for the court to disregard a jury's finding of fact[]. It follows that in a case where legal claims are tried by a jury and equitable claims are tried by a judge, and [those] claims are based on the same facts, the trial judge must follow the jury's implicit or explicit factual determinations in deciding the equitable claims. The trial court must do so in determining both liability and relief on the equitable claims.[20]

According to the Supreme Court, I argued, because the legal and equitable claims did here turn on common issues of fact, the district court was obligated to submit the legal issues to the demanded jury *before* any bench trial on the equitable claims, *and* any determinations by the jury must be adopted by the judge *for* the equitable claims, without re-examination.

As to Cigna's fourth counteraction, Money Had and Received, their brief proposed—without *any* specific citations—that this was among the counterclaims "grounded in the equitable remedy of restitution," and "[b]ecause Cigna brings these counterclaims for recovery of overpayment of benefits under section 502(a) of ERISA, Hackert is not entitled to a jury trial on these issues." The phrase *non sequitur* (Latin for "it does not follow") is defined by Black's as "an inference or conclusion that does not logically follow from the premises." You might recall Cigna's earlier invocation of ERISA 502(a) as the "*exclusive* remedy" to recover self-funded plan benefits, so don't ask me why Cigna was even pursuing the counterclaim of Money Had and Received under the assignment-present scenario. My brief meanwhile demonstrated that there *is* a right to a jury for Money Had and Received per the US Supreme Court: "In England, long prior to the enactment of our first Judiciary Act, common law actions [like] money had and received were resorted to for the recovery of preferential payments by bankrupts.... These actions, like all suits at law, were conducted before juries." (*Granfinanciera, SA v. Nordberg*, 492 U.S. 33, 109 S. Ct. 2782, 106 L. Rd. 2d 26 (1989).) As further confirmation that a jury was apropos to the fourth counterclaim, I pointed out that a

85

section titled "Common Count: Money Had and Received" appeared in the current version of California's Civil Jury Instructions (which, by the way, are abbreviated "CACI" for "California Civil Instructions" and pronounced "Casey"): "[F]or money had and received...juries are instructed...the plaintiff must prove that the defendant received money intended to be used for the benefit of [the plaintiff], that the money was not used for the plaintiff's benefit, and that the defendant has not given the money to the plaintiff." (Judicial Council of California Civil Jury Instructions (CACI) 370.)

My brief went on to revisit that an oral contract may have been formed when I called Cigna Provider Relations, which is a question of fact, i.e., an issue to be determined by the fact-finder, and I had selected a jury, not the judge, to be the fact-finder. I further observed that if there *was* a contract, such an agreement would supersede the otherwise preemptive force of ERISA, citing *Marin General Hosp. v. Modesto & Empire Traction*, 581 F.3d 941 (9th Cir. 2009): "The...state-law claims asserted...all arise out of what was allegedly said during that call."

I also argued it would be a role for the jury to interpret the *factual content* of plan documents when they must be consulted, repeating it should not be a foregone conclusion that there were any overpayments at all: "[T]o not consider the terms of the plan...would be to accept the insurer's overpayment determination at face value." (*PREMIER HEALTH CENTER, PC, supra.*) To that point, I contended a jury was also the proper determinant of whether there was, factually, any *anti*-assignment or assignment-*cancelling* language within the plan documents, as I had alleged.

Since Cigna had worded its counterclaim to read "[t]he disputed claims at issue in this litigation *all* concern...self-funded health benefit plans...governed by...ERISA," my brief noted once again that a jury as fact-finder may identify certain claims as insured or priced by Cigna, and thus not governed by ERISA, and therefore excluded from the counterlitigation by Cigna's own pleading. After all, a claimant is considered to be captain of its own case. (cp. *People v. Yamin*, 45 Misc. 2d 407, 257 N.Y.S.2d 11 (NY: Supreme Court, Kings 1965).)

My brief repeated that it was a material fact to be found whether Cigna had issued Adverse Benefit Determinations to recoup the asserted overpayments per the requirements of 29 CFR.[21]

Lest the court attempt to diminish the jury's capacity in the fifth counterclaim for fraud and sixth for negligent misrepresentation, my brief observed that "[m]ateriality and scienter are both fact-specific issues which should ordinarily be left to the trier of fact." (*In re Apple Computer Securities Litigation*, 886 F.2d 1109 (9th Cir. 1989).) "Except in the rare case where the undisputed facts leave no room for a reasonable difference of opinion, the question of whether a plaintiff's reliance is reasonable is a question of fact." (*City Solutions, Inc. v. Clear Channel*, 365 F.3d 835 (9th Cir. 2004).)

Regarding the seventh counterclaim for Unfair Competition, I noted in parallel to *MEDITERRANEAN BEST FOODS, INC. v. GEVORKYAN*, No. B266800 (Cal. Ct. App. June 5, 2017) that "whether (and to what extent) [counterclaimant] is entitled to equitable relief under Business and Professions Code [§ 17200, et seq.]...*is* a matter left to the sound discretion of the trial court...[*but* i]n exercising such discretion, the trial court is bound by the jury's findings with regard to disputed facts common to the legal and equitable claims...." (Emphasis added.)

Regarding a jury's intersection with the *affirmative* defenses, I quoted back to Judge Mueller another one of her own decisions: "If a counterclaim is presented to a jury, including by assertion of an affirmative defense, the court may defer to the jury's factual findings when ruling on that counterclaim." (*Moreno v. Ross Island Sand & Gravel Co.*, No. 2: 13-cv-00691-KJM-KJN (E.D. Cal. June 30, 2016).)

For its broad application I recounted still another of Judge Mueller's opinions: "It is the jury, not the court, which is the fact-finding body." (*Lopez v. Cook*, No. CIV-S-03-1605 KJM-DAD P (E.D. Cal. June 22, 2011).)

One may ask why these briefs were even requested if the court alone was to ascertain the right to a jury. Theoretically, if I had declined to submit a précis the district court would've been constrained by the same authorities I happened to articulate. In the words of the US Supreme Court, "[E]quation of silence or inaction with waiver is a fiction that has been categorically rejected by this Court when other fundamental rights are at stake." (*Dickey v. Florida*, 398 U.S. 30, 90 S. Ct. 1564, 26 L. Ed. 2d 26 (1970).) But I wasn't going to give Judge Mueller fodder for contravening even The Highest Court in the Land yet again.

Chapter 22

The Final Pretrial Order was issued and it was even worse than I predicted. The concerns I had with this document are best conveyed by highlighting the objections I filed against it, even if in vain. Broadcasting my unwillingness to passively forfeit legal rights, among other complementary citations I observed from *Berry v. Bunnell*, 39 F.3d 1056 (9th Cir. 1994) that because a party may "fail[] to object to the proposed pretrial order" at the lower court, "issues not preserved in [the] pretrial order are eliminated from [the] action [on appeal]."

I thus took Judge Mueller's Pretrial Order to the analytic woodshed. "There are," I wrote, "several omissions and inaccuracies which are prejudicial to counterdefendant. [¶] Counterdefendant objects generally to the non-comprehensive format of the Pretrial Order which only selectively follows the structure of Local Rule 281(a)(2)," the court-prescribed outline of the underlying pretrial statements.

As a touchstone I compared the Pretrial Order here to that in one of Judge Mueller's other recent cases, *FEDERAL DEPOSIT INSURANCE CORPORATION v. Ching*, No. 2: 13-cv-01710-KJM-EFB (E.D. Cal. June 29, 2016), where she systematically adhered to the Rule 281(a)(2) format.

Beyond the general concerns, I objected to the Pretrial Order's rendering of the STATEMENT OF THE CASE which read "Cigna's counterclaims against Hackert derive from the following allegations. Hackert, a surgeon, allegedly represented to Cigna, a healthcare services corporation, that certain Cigna members had authorized Cigna to pay their medical benefits to Hackert.... Cigna contends no such assignment was ever made, and even if it was, the amounts Cigna paid Hackert were greater than what was *contractually* required...." (Emphasis added.)

You might wonder why I would take issue with this since I had been pleading about the possible existence of written, quasi, or oral contracts, but it alarmed me that even at this late hour the judge apparently wasn't understanding counterclaimant's position that "[T]here is no evidence [of] a written, oral, or implied contract...between Hackert and Cigna for assistant surgeon services...."[22] I also had to remonstrate that "Cigna does not actually contend that 'no such assignment was ever made.' To the contrary, Cigna pled that '[p]laintiff <u>must</u> be proceeding as an assignee.'"

I reiterated that Cigna had effectively abandoned its fifth, sixth, and seventh fraud-based counterclaims for gross lack of particularity and specificity, having not grounded its contentions in any tangible patient claims. Whereas the figure of $2,980.41 for the non-fraud claims was at least tabulated in the counterclaim, completely unitemized were the asserted twenty-three thousand odd dollars in damages for the fifth, sixth, and seventh counterclaims, thus making it impossible to prepare a defense against which, and thus barred. To explain that, you'll recall Fed. Rule Civ. Proc. 9(b) states "In alleging fraud...a party must state with particularity the circumstances constituting fraud...." In the words of the Second Circuit's *DiVittorio v. Equidyne Extractive Industries, Inc.*, 822 F.2d 1242 (2d Cir. 1987), "Rule 9(b) is designed to further three goals: (1) providing a defendant fair notice of plaintiff's claim, to enable preparation of defense; (2) protecting a defendant from harm to his reputation or goodwill; and (3) reducing the number of strike suits," defined by Black's as "A suit (esp. a derivative action), often based on no valid claim, brought either for nuisance value or as leverage...." Look familiar? Cigna's counterclaim was from the outset "unmeritorious" as a lawyer would say, intended, I believe, to so frighten me that I assuredly would have dismissed the case early on. Legal hubris.

Returning to my objections to the Pretrial Order, in the section JURISDICTION/VENUE Judge Mueller begged the question: "Jurisdiction is predicated upon 28 U.S.C. § 1331, given Cigna's federal claim. Venue is proper based on 28 U.S.C. § 1441(a)."

Let's look at the text of 28 U.S.C. § 1331: "The district courts shall have original jurisdiction of all civil actions arising under the Constitution, laws, or treaties of the United States."

28 U.S.C. § 1441(a) reads: "Except as otherwise expressly provided by Act of Congress, any civil action brought in a State court of which the district courts of the United States have original jurisdiction, may be removed by the defendant...to the district court of the United

States for the district and division embracing the place where such action is pending."

From Chapter 5 you'll remember it was Cigna that sought to "remove this action from the Superior Court of the State of California...to the United States District Court...pursuant to Title 28, United States Code, section[] 1441(a)" on the basis that I had assignment. My objections to the Pretrial Order thus reiterated that I consistently pled and declared that I was not a[n] assignee of any beneficiary vis-à-vis ERISA, but the district court had "expressly rejected" this assertion, ruling that "Cigna has carried its burden to show Hackert submitted claims as his patients' assignee and would have standing to bring an ERISA action, and the removal was proper." In the present context of Cigna's counterclaim, then, I either must be considered to have assignment unequivocally, or, I argued, Cigna's federal counterclaim must be *dismissed*: "If the court determines at any time that it lacks subject-matter jurisdiction, the court must dismiss the action. Fed. R. Civ. P. 12(h)(3)." (*SAN FRANCISCO HERRING ASSOCIATION, supra.*) And I noted once again, "[W]here all federal claims are eliminated before trial, courts generally should decline to exercise supplemental jurisdiction over remaining state law claims." (*Ashford, supra.*)

Under the UNDISPUTED FACTS section of the Pretrial Order, among other running protestations I raised an objection regarding Judge Mueller's statement that "This court adopted the Magistrate Judge's recommendations in full." An earlier order had remarked that "If the case is tried to a jury, the undisputed facts will be read to the jury." I thus asked Judge Mueller to rephrase the above statement to read "This court adopted the Magistrate Judge's recommendations in full, *finding that Cigna carried its burden to show Hackert submitted claims as his patients' assignee.*" I know, I'm absurd for clinging to the truth.

Perhaps the most treacherous section of the Pretrial Order was *DISPUTED* FACTUAL ISSUES. To give you a sense of the apparent indifference of the court, my pretrial statement had enumerated 54 critical disputed factual issues, many nested with subseries, but here is how Mueller's Pretrial Order read:

DISPUTED FACTUAL ISSUES
The following facts are disputed and will be addressed

at trial:

1. Whether Hackert received assignments of benefits from any Cigna members whose claims are at issue in this action.

2. In the alternative, if Hackert did receive assignments of benefits from the Cigna members, whether the members' health plan obligates Cigna to pay Hackert's bills; and if so, whether Cigna overpaid Hackert.

Lest you think it's routine for a judge to distill a complexity of associated facts into just a couple of points, I again referenced the *Ching* litigation where Judge Mueller had itemized several if not all of the disputed factual issues, and thus objected to the omission from the instant Pretrial Order of the contested factual matters raised by pretrial statement.

The SPECIAL FACTUAL INFORMATION section just read "None," and so I objected that my pretrial statement had demonstrated a reasonable jury might determine that an oral contract was offered and accepted, and that Cigna actually *under*paid the claims asserted to have been *over*paid. I repeated that my pretrial statement invoked estoppel under this section, because, for the vast majority of the claims, Cigna issued Remittance Advices reporting "contractual" adjustments or referencing a "contract." Cigna formally upheld these determinations by written response to several appeals, and to date had issued no amended Remittance Advices. For the vast majority of claims in dispute, Cigna's own billing records therefore indicated that there *was* a contract. Cigna thereby waived its assertion that there was not a contract. I also reargued that Cigna should be estopped from evading any quasi-contract, which, again, is "an obligation...created by the law with*out* regard to the intention of the parties...." (*Unilab, supra*. Emphasis added.)

With respect to the Pretrial Order's DISPUTED EVIDENTIARY ISSUES section, I objected that the court essentially cut-and-paste Cigna's issues from their pretrial statement(s), while reducing mine to 2-line boilerplate.

I objected to the Order's RELIEF SOUGHT section, not necessarily because the court cut-and-paste Cigna's text yet again but more so on wording I believe Cigna was quietly attempting to introduce: "*Damages* in the amount Cigna overpaid Hackert for health care services rendered to Cigna members...." (Emphasis added.) I reminded the court that the counterclaim's original (and unless amended, governing) prayer for relief requested "*monetary* damages" on causes of action where the only potential relief would be *equitable*. In other words, the counterclaim's own wording precluded any award for the ERISA-related causes, unless the court was to allow the somewhat more generic "damages" to creep into the record and encompass "*equitable* restitution."

Regarding the POINTS OF LAW section, the Pretrial Order tersely stated "The court has received the parties' points of law." I observed that in the *Ching* matter, however, Judge Mueller recapitulated each side's points within the Pretrial Order, and, accordingly, I wrote "Counterdefendant thus reserves the right to object to any later attempt to abrogate the content of his pretrial statement with respect to legal or affirmative theories of defense, including citations to statutes, ordinances, regulations, cases, and other authorities."

In part to document the district court judge's cursory handling of my filing, I also objected to the entry of "None" under the Order's ABANDONED ISSUES section since my pretrial statement had abandoned as an affirmative defense "Failure to State a Cause of Action" based on a past writing of Judge Mueller: "The undersigned has sided with what appears to be the majority, and has found that failure to state a claim is not an affirmative defense."

Regarding the Pretrial Order's EXHIBITS, SCHEDULES AND SUMMARIES section, I objected to the court granting Cigna permission to substantially expand its exhibit and discovery list *after* the filing of their pretrial statement(s), based on Local Rule 281(b)(11) which reads: "Only exhibits so listed [in the pretrial statement] will be permitted to be offered at trial." Another indulgence for Cigna, based on their objection to the working Final Pretrial Order that "After the pretrial conference, Hackert advised Cigna's counsel that he continues to dispute the court's finding that he received assignments of benefits from the Cigna patients whose claims are at issue in this litigation." That ironic misquote notwithstanding, Judge Mueller did issue an *Amended* Final Pretrial Order, the tone of which summed up the history and future of the case at large:

> Both parties have filed timely objections to the final
> pretrial order. Hackert takes issue with the order's

summary nature, repeats and expands his legal arguments, and seeks to incorporate more factual detail. Hackert's objections do not provide good cause to amend the order; they are overruled. Cigna proposes three specific amendments[, to amplify their exhibit list and discovery list, and to rephrase how it would be described to the jury]. Good cause appearing, the court incorporates Cigna's proposed amendments...."

Judge Mueller slipped these donatives to Cigna via footnote: "Hackert's [exhibit] list provides some additional details as the court directed. Cigna's list includes far more than the one additional exhibit it suggested it would add."

Another insidious footnote read "Because this order lists as a 'disputed fact' whether Hackert received any assignment of benefits from the relevant Cigna patients, the court approves Cigna's request to change the wording in [its] exhibit list to pertain to 'all 32 claims.'"

The court was effectively giving Cigna a full rewrite of its counterclaim, without formal amendment and the attendant opportunity for an answer. Initially limited to 18 claims, the non-fraud counteractions now included all 32 of those in my original complaint, but much more consequentially, the fraud allegations previously soulless were now embodied.

When we hear the word "fiat" we might first envision the automobile company, but its underlying meaning within the lexicon is "an authoritative or arbitrary order."[23] What can I say? Bleak House.

Chapter 23

A mere two weeks before the trial was to commence Judge Mueller finally issued an order regarding the jury demand:

"The court finds Hackert is entitled to a jury trial on a threshold factual issue and on two claims[, t]he fraud and negligent misrepresentation claims. [¶] … [¶]

"The threshold question is whether Cigna members assigned their benefits to Hackert.

"If the Cigna members did assign their benefits to Hackert, that finding triggers Cigna's first, second, third and fourth claims, which seek to recover Cigna's alleged overpayments based on these assignments. There is no right to a jury trial on these counterclaims because Cigna seeks only equitable remedies in the form of a refund of the overpaid amounts, and the counterclaims are brought under section 502(a)(3) of ERISA.

"Alternatively, if Hackert did not receive benefits assignments, that finding triggers Cigna's fifth, sixth and seventh counterclaims….

"[Hackert's] demand for a jury trial on all other claims and issues is DENIED."

Chapter 24

In medical school our third-year radiology instructor was vintage, a treasure of knowledge and insight from a bygone era. Some of the students complained that he wasn't actually teaching radiology, but that's because his style was to present a concept and then show through vignettes just why the reader of films needed the given lesson in the armamentarium. One theme was *Always Consider the Alternatives*, and the point developed was that a broad differential must be kept in mind because anything is possible.

I couldn't help but think back to that lecture as I tried to understand what was happening in this case. Had the court been purchased? Perhaps the judge was saying "*Pro pers* aren't welcome in our club"? Maybe the judiciary has a grudge against physicians? I don't know. With the trial date approaching, all I could do was prepare for battle.

Judge Mueller's latest order stated "The parties *may* file trial briefs of up to twenty (20) pages," and I found it disconcerting that Cigna would file no brief at all. The questions swirled again. Corruption? Overconfidence on Cigna's part? *Budgetary* limits handed down from the corner office? Maybe the abacus sliders at Headquarters told these lawyers they weren't going authorize any more funds than absolutely necessary for what was a lost cause. Although Judge Mueller's court was partial, the Ninth Circuit would surely respect the law on appeal, wouldn't it?

For my trial brief I used up the last corner of the twentieth page to document the affront to justice in progress.

Chapter 25

I introduced my trial brief recalling *US v. Eatinger*, 902 F.2d 1383 (9th Cir. 1990) which instructs that "Pro se petitioners' arguments must be liberally construed." The remaining substance was also largely reiterative but the force of the primacy and recency effect is classic psychology, if Judge Mueller was going to be reading the brief at all.

Channeling the *Zumbrun* opinion, I pled that because the court approved Cigna's request to change the wording in its exhibit list to pertain to "all 32 claims" only after pretrial statements had been submitted, the Court foreclosed any opportunity I would have had to "intelligently meet" Cigna's charges as to the additional 14 claims.

I added citations to avoid dullness and reinforce the arguments. "Whether parties have reached a contractual agreement and on what terms are questions for the fact finder when conflicting versions of the parties' negotiations require a determination of credibility." (*Hebberd-Kulow Enterprises, Inc. v. Kelomar, Inc.*, 218 Cal. App. 4th 272, 159 Cal. Rptr. 3d 869 (Ct. App. 2013).) "Since...[the] common law [claims]...must go to the jury, [the] equitable claims must also await the jury's decision, at least as to factual questions common to both." (*Hilton v. Mumaw*, 522 F.2d 588 (9th Cir. 1975).) "[M]ateriality is a subject for the consideration of a jury." (*Maryland Ins. Co. v. Ruden's Administrator*, 10 U.S. 338, 3 L. Ed. 242 (1810).) "The issue of...liability *vel non*[24] in law and equity must be tried to a jury. If subsequent or separate factual issues respecting equitable relief arise, it may be that those issues are tried to the bench." (*Addington v. US AIRLINE PILOTS ASSOCIATION*, No. CV 08-1633-PHX-NVW (consolidated) (D. Ariz. Feb. 17, 2009).) "Inequitable conduct resides in failure to disclose material information, or submission of false material information, with an intent to deceive, and those two elements, materiality and intent, must be proven by clear and convincing evidence." (*FootBALANCE SYSTEM INC. v. ZERO GRAVITY INSIDE, INC.*, No. 15-CV-1058 JLS (DHB) (S.D. Cal. Sept. 5, 2017).)

Recapping the record, I confronted the court for permitting

Cigna's diametric pleadings regarding the assignment status. A party "cannot advance one version of the facts in its pleadings, conclude that its interests would be better served by a different version, and amend its pleadings to incorporate that version, safe in the belief that the trier of fact will never learn of the change in stories." (*United States v. McKeon*, 738 F.2d 26 (2d Cir. 1984).) "[T]his is notably true when, in consequence of the intrusion into the case of a new or intervening contention...it comes about that the pleader's interest will be served the better by his abandonment of his originally taken factual stance." (*Raulie v. United States*, 400 F.2d 487 (10th Cir. 1968).) "The trial judge may rationally evaluate the bearing upon a position ultimately taken in litigation by a party to a suit, of an inconsistent, or even diametrically opposite position by him theretofore assumed with respect to a material factual issue." (*Id.*) "A pleading prepared by an attorney is an admission by one presumptively authorized to speak for his principal." (*Kunglig Jarnvagsstyrelsen v. Dexter & Carpenter*, 32 F.2d 195 (2d Cir. 1929).) In the eyes of the Court itself, I continued, counterdefendant has assignment of benefits: "On the motion to remand, plaintiff asserted that he was not an assignee, an assertion expressly rejected by the District Court."

I turned once again to US Supreme Court in *Taylor v. Sturgell*, 553 U.S. 880, 128 S. Ct. 2161, 171 L. Ed. 2d 155 (2008): "Issue preclusion...bars successive litigation of an issue of fact or law actually litigated and resolved in a valid court determination essential to the prior judgment, even if the issue recurs in the context of a different claim. By preclud[ing] parties from contesting matters that they have had a full and fair opportunity to litigate, th[is] doctrine[] protect[s] against the expense and vexation attending multiple lawsuits, conserv[es] judicial resources, and foste[rs] reliance on judicial action by minimizing the possibility of inconsistent decisions."

I reminded Judge Mueller that per such cases as *Omar v. Sea-Land Service, Inc.*, 813 F.2d 986 (9th Cir. 1987), "A trial court may dismiss a claim sua sponte[25] under Fed.R.Civ.P. 12(b)(6)," and "[s]uch a dismissal may be made without notice where the claimant cannot possibly win relief."

I also noted that the court incorrectly identified Money Had and Received as an action "brought in equity" for which there is not a right to a jury trial, directing Judge Mueller back to *Granfinanciera*:

"[I]nsofar as the complaint requests a money judgment it presents a claim which is unquestionably legal." But just in case the district court considered that Supreme Court opinion obsolete, I cited a 2004 cross-reference from the California Court of Appeal, *Wisden v. Superior Court*, 21 Cal. Rptr. 3d 523, 124 Cal. App. 4th 750 (Ct. App. 2004): "Based upon the historical analysis in *Granfinanciera*, it appears beyond debate that...the right to trial by jury existed at common law in an action to recover an alleged fraudulent conveyance of a determinate sum of money... We must necessarily conclude...that the same right to trial by jury...exists today." Lastly I cited the California Supreme Court in *Mains v. City Title Insurance Co.*, 34 Cal. 2d 580, 212 P.2d 873 (1949): although Money Had and Received is "governed by principles of equity[,¶] such an action is one at law."

I then underscored the problem of subject-matter jurisdiction, recounting that the recent order of the court set an algorithm by which the jury will first determine the threshold question of whether I received assignment of benefits. I pointed out that if the jury were to find I did not, the *proper* procedure would be to remand the entire case, and not allow Cigna to continue in federal court on its fraud-based counterclaims. Having "expressly rejected" my assertion that I was not an assignee, the court obviated jury determination of that question at summary judgment on my complaint. I reminded Judge Mueller that from *Anderson v. Liberty Lobby* as previously cited by her own court:

> [S]ummary judgment will not lie if the dispute about a material fact is genuine, that is, if the evidence is such that a reasonable jury could return a verdict for the nonmoving party. [T]he availability of summary judgment turn[s] on whether a proper jury question was presented.
>
> [A]t the summary judgment stage the judge's function is not [her]self to weigh the evidence and determine the truth of the matter but to determine whether there is a genuine issue for trial.
>
> The inquiry performed is the threshold inquiry of determining whether there is the need for a trial — whether, in other words, there are any genuine factual issues that properly can be resolved only by a finder of

fact....

Logically, I wrote, if a jury empanelled to hear Cigna's *counter*claim were to determine that I did not have assignment, this court *must* have improperly granted Cigna's motion for summary judgment on my complaint, the antithesis of which would have been to approve my motion to remand at that time, as each hinged on the same threshold question. To educate Judge Mueller, if necessary, I rehearsed Fed. R. Civ. P. 54(b): "[A]ny order or other decision, however designated, that adjudicates fewer than all the claims or the rights and liabilities of fewer than all the parties does not end the action as to any of the claims or parties and may be revised at any time before the entry of a judgment adjudicating all the claims and all the parties' rights and liabilities." A federal court, I noted, "ha[s] an independent obligation to address sua sponte whether [it] has subject-matter jurisdiction." (*Dittman v. California*, 191 F.3d 1020, 1025 (9th Cir. 1999).)

I also revisited an anticipated dispute regarding the summoning of C. Leavitt, Esq., author of Cal. Code Regs., tit. 28, § 1300.71, subd. (a)(3) in the former capacity of Assistant Chief Counsel to the DMHC, one and the same as Cigna's lead attorney. By reference to *US v. State*, No. 2: 70-CV-09213-RSM (W.D. Wash. Mar. 2, 2017) I brought to Judge Mueller's attention that per the Rules of Professional Conduct, "[a] lawyer shall not act as advocate at a trial in which the lawyer is likely to be a necessary witness.... (RPC, Rule 3.7, Lawyer as Witness)." Cigna, I furthermore noted, had neglected to file any opposing motion *in limine*—Latin for "on the doorstep," as in the final approach to the courthouse.

Chapter 26

"Calling civil case 15-1248," the clerk announced. There was no "all rise" kind of thing. No need. We were all old friends here. Judge Mueller opened with "housekeeping" issues and conferred with the parties regarding how they wished to word the jury instructions on the threshold question of assignment. Disregarded of course were the proposed jury instructions I had filed, against which Cigna filed none at all.

Because it was Cigna's case as counterclaimant, the court heard Mr. Leavitt's input first. He wasted no time inverting his prior position: "[T]here are no written documents and no evidence to support that an assignment actually occurred."

No, you can't zap your opponent with a truth taser right on the spot, even though if it were a shouting match, I might have yelled "Sounds like you've forgotten the declaration you wrote for Cheri Barron to sign, testifying that the medical claims *were* submitted under assignment? How about your earlier pleadings like 'Plaintiff's claim that he did not receive any assignments of benefits appears to be *un*true,' or 'Plaintiff <u>must</u> be proceeding as an assignee'"?

When Judge Mueller turned to me, I said "Well, your Honor, I think the entire instruction is prejudicial because it effectively sidesteps the...legal doctrine of collateral estoppel, more specifically, issue preclusion."

Mueller actually responded: "Because you think I have decided that already on the motion to remand and summary judgment?"

"Correct, your Honor."

Judge Mueller replied, "I've determined that that focused question, at least initially, should go to a jury. I understand you object. I think your trial brief makes that clear. And I'm overruling that objection...."

"I must object on the record for preservation because the very essence of a motion for summary judgment is to make a legal determination where no reasonable jury could find in favor of the

103

nonmoving party....[¶] ... [¶] And here's the point if I didn't make it clear. Really the first line in this type of instruction should read: Did Cigna plead, previously plead, that Hackert had assignment of benefits with respect to Hackert's complaint against Cigna. Next line, did the Court concur with Cigna's pleading that Hackert had assignment of benefits with respect to Hackert's complaint against Cigna. And my point again is issue preclusion, it is already well-established in the record that Cigna did plead –"

"Dr. Hackert, you have preserved that issue. And I'm overruling that objection, and the jury should not hear any question, any comment, any argument that references collateral estoppel or preclusion. Understood?"

"No, your Honor. I don't agree with that."

"That is my order to you. You've preserved. There's a transcript. You can take this to the appellate court. That is not the question the jury is being asked to answer. The jury is a fact finder, and you want them to reconsider legal questions that I have resolved. And so you are ordered, and if you don't comply with that order, there will be consequences...."

I had already prepared for the possibility of ending up in the brig before this whole thing was over.

After a few less noteworthy interchanges I said, "I would like to move at this time for a mistrial based on judicial bias."

"...I'm telling you you've made that argument" Judge Mueller retorted, "you have a record, you can appeal me once we're done with this proceeding. Your briefs also cover the issue...."

"Your Honor, you may not recall, but this court, your court, it was the magistrate judge under your guidance in a pleading said the Court expressly rejects Hackert's assertion that he does not have assignment with respect to ERISA."

"I do recall footnote 2. I don't supervise the magistrate judge. Magistrate judges are independent judicial officers. They prepare findings and recommendations that are published. I don't talk behind the scenes with the magistrate judge. The parties have chances to object. I have considered your argument that footnote 2 supports your preclusion argument. I just don't think that's a fair characterization of the record. You may appeal me on that when this proceeding is done, but at this point this Court did not engage in fact-finding based on that stray comment in a footnote on summary judgment. So is there anything else that you think makes me biased against you?"

"Just for the record because you asked, your Honor, you did adopt in full, as the key phrase, you as the presiding judge adopted in full the magistrate judge's findings and recommendations."

"I understand that. And I've gone back and I've considered that argument. And summary judgment, courts on summary judgment do not resolve factual questions. Courts decide whether or not a reasonable fact-finder could decide a question one way or the other. And the Court previously has not engaged in fact-finding in this case."

"Thank you, your Honor. And if it's an appropriate time, for efficiency sake, there is a logical conclusion if the jury were to find that Hackert does not have assignment, then what that calls for, of course, is to remand the case, as argued in the trial brief."

"I understand that argument, and we'll get there after the first phase."

"Thank you, your Honor. I appreciate that."

"The Court's tentative thought is that I have supplemental jurisdiction, and it would be highly inefficient to remand at that stage."

"Your Honor, thank you for raising that point. You may also recall the citation -- I can read it to you if you like -- that says a federal court generally should not maintain jurisdiction when all federal questions have been eliminated. That is to say if there would only be supplemental jurisdiction with respect to, for example, state law causes, the case should still be remanded."

"I'm well familiar with that basic principle. Depending on how the first question or questions are answered, I'll allow you to argue. But addressing the efficiency question, is it really fair to a state court and is it the correct decision legally to remand? But we're not there yet. We'll cross that bridge when we come to it."

Before leaving the topic I conveyed to the judge that the process unfolding was "akin to the concept of double jeopardy." The Fifth Amendment protects against being criminally prosecuted twice for the same act. Here, the court had earlier ruled that Cigna carried its burden to show I had assignment, but was now trying me on the supposition that I did not.

Chapter 27

Next was the *voir dire*. Latin doesn't have a monopoly on legalese—this a French phrase meaning "to speak the truth." As Black's Law Dictionary explains, it's "a preliminary examination of a prospective juror by a judge or lawyer to decide whether the prospect is qualified and suitable to serve on a jury." Prospective jurors may be dismissed for either cause, or up to a certain number, by "peremptory challenge," that is, at the will of a party.

Judge Mueller was expert in her questioning of the juror-candidates who filed in on the clerk's cue: Does anyone know any of the parties or witnesses? Has anyone heard anything about this case? Is there anyone who would find it difficult or impossible to serve as a juror?

Each prospective juror was then asked to introduce him- or herself and respond to questions about work, family, military service, prior jury experience, and so on. Mueller gave each one a thorough examination, including about any medical billing or claims issues they may themselves have had.

My impression was that our body of potential jurors did the citizenry proud. It truly felt like an honor having these people all but share their life stories for my sake, and I can say mine because I was the one who had asked them to be there.

Judge Mueller then posed a just-to-be-sure sort of question, "Has anyone thought of *anything* that makes them think that they could not be fair in this case if you were seated ultimately as a juror?," and one candidate started to show some cracks, Prospective Juror # 13: "My girlfriend is a medical coder, and we have several discussions in reference to certain things that may be prohibitive. I'm not sure...."

Mueller scoured the candidate: "[W]ould you say you have strong opinions about the players in that system, in the medical billing and insurance system?"

"It's a possibility, yeah."

"All right. So here you have an insurance company on the one side, a doctor on the other. Would you think that you might be likely to put the thumb on the scale for one or the other based on what you know?"

"It's hard to determine that at this point but –"

Judge Mueller interrupted to explain the concept of impermissible bias, then continued: "Do you think given what you know based on hearing about your girlfriend's medical coding job that you would be unable to set that aside and decide the case based only on what happens here in court and what I tell you the law is?"

"I'd try."

"All right. Do you have some doubt?"

"Little bit...."

"I'm going to ask the parties to come to a sidebar," Judge Mueller informed the incipient panel. "We turn on white noise so that I can have a discussion with them. You may stand and stretch, but please don't talk amongst yourselves because the court reporter does need to take down what we're talking about. And I'm going to ask if they have any challenges for cause and also if they want me to ask more questions."

Naturally Mr. Leavitt challenged Prospective Juror # 13, and he was called into the principal's office. Under cover of the white noise machine and out of earshot of the other prospective jurors, Judge Mueller questioned him further. "We want to make certain we understand what you're saying. We appreciate your expressing concern about your ability to be fair. Are you specifically saying that as between an insurance company and a doctor you might tend to favor one or the other?"

"I think I would."

"Which side would you favor?"

"The doctor's side. Sorry."

Judge Mueller gave Prospective Juror # 13 his walking papers and announced "I'll bring a new juror into the box and have them answer all the questions." After vetting the replacement candidate, Muller invited the parties to exercise their peremptory strikes by paper ballot, and then, following a short recess announced, "It appears we have a jury."

Chapter 28

Following a lunch break but before reseating the jury, Judge Mueller resumed by sharing her revisions to the jury instructions. "Any final objections?," she asked.

"None from Cigna, your Honor," Mr. Leavitt said.

"Dr. Hackert?"

"If we turn back to the first version as provided this morning on page 5-"

"So that's now no longer before the Court," Judge Mueller interjected.

"Well, you requested objections, your Honor. And so with respect to line 23, 'An assignment does not have to be in a particular form,' the objection is that counterdefendant did request for that to remain in the instructions, and it does not appear to be in the instructions."

"It is not in the instructions at this point. I am including the instruction to alert the jury to the nature of the decision it has to make. I do reserve the right to give that same instruction again and supplement it depending on the evidence that comes in."

"Thank you, your Honor."

"And so that objection is overruled for now," Judge Muller pronounced in case there was any doubt.

After covering a few other items the nod was given to the clerk: "Let's bring the jury in."

Judge Muller introduced the case:

> Cigna is a health services company that sells health insurance and health plans to employers and consumers throughout the country. Cigna also administers self-funded plans for employers and unions, and these plans are governed by ERISA, the Employee Retirement Income Security Act.
>
> Dr. Hackert is an assistant surgeon that has provided services to Cigna members. Dr. Hackert originally claimed that Cigna underpaid him on 32 claims for

benefit payments based on services he provided to Cigna's members. Cigna takes the position that it overpaid Dr. Hackert for many of these services and seeks to recoup the allegedly overpaid amounts.

Cigna argues in part that Dr. Hackert misrepresented that he was entitled to receive the payments on behalf of Cigna's members when, in fact, the members never assigned Dr. Hackert those rights.Not sure how you took that synopsis, but maybe you find it just as prejudicial as I, the way the judge left in the jury's mind the notion that "when, in fact, the members never assigned Dr. Hackert those rights."

Mueller then provided the jurors their immediate charge: "The sole question presented to the jury at this phase of the trial is whether the identified Cigna members assigned to Dr. Hackert their right to receive medical benefit payments from Cigna. An assignment occurs when a party to a contract transfers his or her rights under that contract for valuable consideration to a third party."After running through some other logistical preliminaries, Judge Mueller gave the podium to Mr. Leavitt for his opening statement, abridged here:

The question and the evidence that you're going to be asked about is was there an assignment of benefits that would allow Dr. Hackert to bill either the employer or Cigna for the services he provided.And we believe there was not.

So how does an assignment of benefits work? Well, you have the employer who has a self-funded plan that's being administered by Cigna, and they have employees who are covered under that plan. When an employee goes to a doctor or a hospital, or any other provider, that doctor and hospital will ask the employee, now patient, to sign what's called an assignment of benefits. And as it indicates, an assignment of benefits is an authorization from the patient for the doctor to directly bill the employer. The benefits belong to the employee.

If there is no assignment of benefits, if the patient never signed a piece of paper saying you can bill my employer directly my self-funded plan to pay for your services, if that doesn't occur, then the doctor is not

110

allowed to bill for the services. You don't get to bill for services without an assignment of benefits.

So we have this situation here where there have been 29 claims that were paid to Dr. Hackert. And through the course of the litigation, the evidence will show that Cigna, on behalf of these employers, learned that Dr. Hackert never got assignment of benefits.

And where is this evidence going to come from? It's really one source. One of it is Dr. Hackert will admit, he will testify under oath, as he has done in the past, that he never received an assignment of benefits.

[I]n addition to admitting that, there are no documents that you will see from any patient saying that they assigned the benefits.

As Mr. Leavitt concluded, Judge Mueller advised the jury, "Now Dr. Hackert also has the right to give an opening statement...."

I took the podium and without saying "Damn the consequences!," began to give the other side of the story, attempting to convey to the jury that the evidence would show how Cigna removed the case to federal court maintaining I had assignment, but Judge Mueller interrupted: "[T]his is procedural history. It is not relevant to the issue being tried."

"Counterdefendant takes exception for the record."

"Your issue is preserved," replied the court.

Considering a bailiff still hadn't cuffed and dragged me away, I resumed:

"Thank you, your Honor. And so providing that counterdefendant is allowed to actually present the evidence, what you'll see as a jury is that Cigna pled, that is to say, in their court papers, they argued Dr. Hackert has assignment. He must have assignment. And the Court has to make a decision, and the Court ultimately concurred. They said well, Cigna has carried its burden to show that Hackert has assignment."

"Dr. Hackert does not speak for the Court," Judge Mueller interjected. "I'm not taking a position, but I'm just -- Dr. Hackert has been instructed the procedural history that you're reviewing and summarizing is not relevant to the question that's currently before the jury. You have preserved your right with other documents you filed with the Court, but you do not speak for the Court. You are not the one to tell the jury what the Court previously has decided."

"Thank you, your Honor." Still no vaudeville hook, so I continued. "[W]as Cigna defrauded?...Did I pull the wool over Cigna's eyes to indicate to them that I had assignment? Now, the evidence will show that my testimony has been consistent throughout this entire matter. And, namely, that is the evidence will show that I was the first to say that I do not have and did not have assignment. The phrase used was vis-à-vis. It's a French phrase. I don't speak French, but my understanding is it's a way to signal in a formal sense with respect to. With respect to ERISA, I don't have a formal assignment of benefits, but I was submitting claims on behalf of patients as a courtesy according to what are called industry standards. That's a term, if you haven't come across it, it just means that's how it's done, according to my understanding.

"The evidence will show that there are court opinions we'll look at, in other words, not my opinion but court decisions as the evidence is reviewed [which] will substantiate that perspective.

"So at this point, the last really issue, last kind of concept I'd like to import to you, the judge explained that assignment as a concept is one that is contractual. And that was a formal instruction you received. There are different types of contracts. And as you may or may not know, one is a formal express written contract. The other is where there's an understanding. That's called an implied contract.

"And my perspective, as the evidence will show, is that if anything that I have indicated by a check box on a claim form, if it is a misrepresentation in the sense of not being true with respect to ERISA, it nonetheless was an implied contract for assignment from the patients on whose behalf I was submitting claims and, in fact, at my own expense to go through the claims processing system.

"So those are the opening remarks I have with respect to this, we would say, []threshold question. Do I have assignment? Yes or no. That is the decision that our [j]udge, [Judge] Mueller[,] is going to ask you to make before we proceed further in this trial. Thank you very much."

Judge Mueller then explained, "[W]e'll turn now to Cigna to begin with presentation of evidence." "Mr. Leavitt, do you have evidence to present at this time?"

"At this time we'd like to call Dr. Hackert to the stand."

Once I was sworn in Mr. Leavitt said, "Take a look at what has been marked as Exhibit 1-1." It appeared to be a *blank* CMS 1500. This document, a completely empty claim form, wasn't even in Cigna's final exhibit list, and thus hypothetically couldn't be offered at trial, but Judge Mueller had just given Cigna late hour carte blanche to augment its exhibits however it wanted and it would've been counterproductive to object in front of the jury. But I understood the strategy. What could be clearer than a blank form?

Mr. Leavitt asked, "Are you familiar with filling out this form when you submit claims on behalf of patients?"

An acquaintance once commented, "Lawyers think...*differently.*" To me everything was a presumed trap, and so, not intending to be difficult, I answered "No" with the proviso that I utilized a billing service and did not myself fill out the forms or submit the claims. I also pointed out that some claims may have been posted electronically.

Mr. Leavitt marched on, asking if I recognized a series of actual claims among his exhibits. I had to reply, "They are, of course, fairly heavily redacted, but my name appears in the identification box and so, generally speaking they look to be among the claim forms that my billing service submitted."

After the court admitted the series of claims, Mr. Leavitt asked "Now, Dr. Hackert, with regard to these claims, did you receive assignment of benefits from the patients whose services you provided?"

I initially answered with a truthful "I don't know," but Mr. Leavitt persisted, and so, riding the line between truth and "consequences," I said "[I]f you're asking for a yes or no answer, strictly speaking yes or no, the answer is yes, because Cigna itself has already pled, meaning it has already argued that I have assignment. And so I believe that I have assignment for these claims."

"Okay. What is the basis of your belief?" But then Mr. Leavitt caught himself. "Let me back up."

There's a concept in law called "opening the door," described by Black's as "an attorney's conduct or questions that render otherwise inadmissible evidence or objectionable questions admissible." Although I would've happily recounted in full the basis of that belief, Mr. Leavitt rephrased the question before I could answer: "Did you have each patient whose claim you submitted sign a document called assignment of benefits?"

"No."

Did you get paid based on your submission of these claims that you have identified as being accurate?"

"There were number of claims that were not paid anything. They were we would call it a zero pay claim. I don't know this one whether it was paid or not."

"Do you know that the reason you were paid, if at all, was because you said on your claim form that you had obtained a signature from the patient indicating you had an assignment of benefits?"

"Well, it sounds like you're asking my opinion."

"No, I was asking your knowledge."

"Well, my knowledge is that it's the industry standard to submit claims on behalf of patients. That was -- when this claim was generated, there was no question in my mind that that's just how it's done. And so that's, what you see in front of you is, from my perspective, just what is done as an industry standard in medical billing."

"You believe that doctors routinely misrepresent on their claims the information that they've certified as being true; is that correct? Do I understand your testimony?"

I turned to the dais, "Your Honor, obviously I have to object because the question, it forms a legal conclusion within its substance, and it must be –"

As with most of my other objections, Judge Mueller interrupted and directed the witness to respond.

"Okay. My understanding is it is not routine for physicians to misrepresent claim information."

Mr. Leavitt then asked me to read the *back* of the claim form to the jury.

"[I]t's very small print, but it appears to read, 'Notice: Any person who knowingly files a statement...containing any misrepresentation or any false, incomplete, or misleading information may be guilty of a criminal act punishable under the law and may be subject to civil penalties.'"

"Were you aware that on the back of the form that had your signature was this reminder of the importance of the truthfulness and accuracy of the information contained on the front of the form?"

Growing weary of attempting to object to the judge I just said, "Really I don't think the question is very fair because you're presuming that I knowingly misrepresented, and my testimony is that I did not knowingly misrepresent anything."

"You didn't sign the forms indicating that you had assignment of benefits?"

"Your Honor, I really think this is an asked and answered scenario," and she seemed to agree, commenting "I think that's fair. I think at this point you can move on, Mr. Leavitt," but then decided to call for the midafternoon break.

After the jury was excused, Judge Mueller asked Mr. Leavitt how much more time he anticipated needing. "[H]e testified he didn't have the assignment of benefits. That's what I need. I think I'm done."

"All right," said Judge Mueller, "So, Dr. Hackert, I guess the message is be ready in 15 minutes to present any case you wish to present."

Chapter 29

After the recess Judge Mueller asked Mr. Leavitt, "Have you concluded with the presentation of evidence?"

"I think I'm going to call the Cigna witness to authenticate those electronic claims as being provided so that we can get all of Exhibit 1 into evidence."

I took the opportunity to bring to the court's attention that it had not allowed me to cross-examine myself, which could have been important technically because of certain rules of questioning.

"You will not cross. You'll put on your case and defense," replied Judge Mueller.

"If you'll allow me leading questions that are typically not allowed on a routine witness but on a cross-examinee, yes. So if you'll allow me —"

Mueller interrupted, "That's what I'm saying. If you want to do headline subject matters."

"I want to make sure I'm not waiving a right by not cross-examining myself right now. That's all."

"Agreed no right waived if Dr. Hackert doesn't follow up on your exam?

"Agreed," said Mr. Leavitt.

The jury was ushered in and Mr. Leavitt said, "At this time we would call Cheri Baron."

Mr. Leavitt ran through a series of pre-canned questions, like "How long have you been with Cigna?," to which she replied "For 26 years."

Later attempting to marionette Ms. Baron outright, the script wearied even the judge who finally said, "This is your witness, and the attorney is not testifying. Just a reminder. I know the jury knows that, but open-ended questions." As Black's explains, the leading questions Mr. Leavitt was using "suggest[] the answer to the person being interrogated" which invite "a mere 'yes' or 'no'" reply and "are generally allowed only in cross-examination."

Trial courts are "urge[d]...to limit the use of leading questions to non-controversial or background areas — leading questions must not be allowed in controverted substantive areas where the jury must weigh the evidence and make credibility determinations. [A] trial advocate who is allowed leading questions can both testify for the witness and argue the client's case by the use of leading questions. This practice must not be allowed." (*Stine v. Marathon Oil Co.*, 976 F.2d 254 (5th Cir. 1992).) The Ninth Circuit warns that "A district court will be reversed on the basis of improper leading questions...if the judge's action...amounted to, or contributed to, the denial of a fair trial." (*US v. Archdale*, 229 F.3d 861 (9th Cir. 2000).)

Was there indication on bills submitted by Dr. Hackert that he had obtained written assignment of benefits from each of the 29 patients?"

"There was, yes. There was indication that there was an assignment of benefits."

This testimony deceptively appears to be consistent Baron's earlier declaration opposing my motion to remand, the only difference being that Cigna was now arguing that I did *not* actually have assignment whereas previously they advanced this same testimony as stand-alone evidence that I *did*.

Leavitt then asked Baron to authenticate that seven of the claims were submitted electronically but conveyed the equivalent information as a paper version.

"It's actually the same information," she obliged. "It's just in a different format because of the electronic version."

"And for each claim, did Dr. Hackert state that he had an assignment of benefits?"

"Yes. The assignment of benefits was always yes."

I was then given the opportunity to cross-examine the witness. In double standard, however, Judge Mueller blocked my efforts to introduce components of the earlier docket like Cigna's adamant pleadings that I *had* assignment, and the court's confirmation of which, even though properly admissible.

Any such indirect evidence would preliminarily be considered "hearsay," which the Federal Rules of Evidence define at 801(c) as "a statement that: [¶] (1) the declarant does not make while testifying at the current trial or hearing; and [¶] (2) a party offers in evidence to prove the truth of the matter asserted in the statement." There are nonetheless several formal exceptions, including one for public records, and court documents are public records. Fed. R. Evid. 803, for instance, titled "Exceptions to the Rule Against Hearsay," reads at 803(8): "Public Records. A record or statement of a public office if [¶] ...it sets out [¶] in a civil case...factual findings from a legally authorized investigation...."

As I began to ask witness Barron if she recognized her own declaration in the exhibit binder, Judge Mueller stepped in: "Why would this witness be in a position to answer questions about this exhibit?"

"The reason why," I pointed out, "is that a party's statement in a pleading can be used against that party," drawing on *US v. Bakshinian*, 65 F. Supp. 2d 1104 (C.D. Cal. 1999).

"Well, let's do this. First of all, we're still in Cigna's case, and Cigna presented this witness."

"This would be *cross*-examination, correct?," I persisted.

"It's cross-examination within the scope," the court replied.

"Yes, your Honor. No question it's within the scope of the question of whether or not –"

Judge Mueller cut me off: "Well, just pose the question. What's the question you want to ask this witness?"

"Ms. Baron, I'd like to ask did you testify that Dr. Hackert had assignment of benefits in or attached to Cigna's opposition to Hackert's motion to remand?...."

"I'm afraid I don't understand."

Hearing Baron's live testimony with Mr. Leavitt confirmed my suspicion that she may have been just an innocent placeholder witness whose job was to answer softball questions and sign off on declarations but who didn't have too much real involvement.

I tried to ask her if she recalled Cigna filing an opposition to my motion to remand, though unfortunately not particularly clearly. "I'm sorry. I don't know the answer to that question," she replied.

"[M]y recollection is that you provided an affidavit...." After a moment I was able to give her the specific exhibit number: "Are you able to locate that, Ms. Baron? It sounds like you may not even recall, but if your memory is refreshed by looking at the document, it's entitled 'Affidavit of Cheri Baron in Support of Cigna's Opposition to

Plaintiff's Motion to Remand'; correct?"

"That's what this says, yes."

"Do you have a recollection at this point of preparing that document?"

"No, because I didn't prepare it."

Although I presumed as much, the jury wouldn't necessarily have been aware that Cheri Baron's "affidavit" was written by the attorneys and then just autographed by her as the "declarant."

"Okay. I'd like you to turn, if you would, within that document...." I gave her the sub-exhibit number. "It's only a couple pages away.... And if I could read for you. I'm going to ask you to verify whether or not this is what that page says--"

Mueller interrupted: "Why don't you first clarify that she now recognizes this document."

"Well, you may have said that you don't recognize it because you did not prepare it. Did I hear correctly?"

"I didn't prepare it, but I did sign it, because my signature's there."

"Yes. And that was my next question because it says, quote, 'I can confirm that —'"

As I zeroed in, Mr. Leavitt objected. "He is trying to read a declaration in instead of using it for impeachment purposes by first asking if the document is accurate and correct."

"All right. You can start with that threshold question," resolved Judge Mueller.

"I'll attempt to complete these foundational questions," I minded the court. "I know you said that you don't actually recognize the document after all, but let me ask you in its general appearance, does it appear to you to be typical of such an affidavit?"

"It has that appearance."

"Do you have any reason to question its trustworthiness as a document that is in the court's files?"

Judge Mueller turned her gaze to Mr. Leavitt: "I believe Ms. Baron just said that's her signature. So is there a dispute that this is an affidavit she signed?"

"No," Leavitt conceded.

"So I think this is an affidavit Ms. Baron acknowledges she signed," Judge Mueller said.

"[Y]our Honor," I continued, "at some point I would like to move into evidence the entire Exhibit but, at minimum, the pages of th[is] Exhibit, that is, the docket entry that corresponds to the title of Cheri Baron's affidavit."

"I understand the document you're referring to. Are you, as Mr. Leavitt has suggested, trying to impeach?"

"Yes, your Honor."

"So what's the impeachment question?"

"Ms. Baron," I asked, "would you agree that you just applied your signature to this document without even actually having prepared its contents?"

"I would say that's fair to say because it's a legal document, and I'm not a lawyer. I'm a claims processor, and I work for Cigna Healthcare. So that's fair to say that I did not prepare this legal document."

I then had the witness turn to a neighboring passage: "It does say, the very first line before paragraph 1 reads, 'I, Cheri Baron, hereby declare,' does it not?"

"It does."

"And paragraph number 2, it says, 'I have personal knowledge of the matters stated herein,' does it not?"

"It does."

"Is it your testimony that Dr. Hackert had assignment of benefits with respect to the claims in question?"

"On the claims that I did review, there was an assignment of benefits."

"And do you have any question to -- do you have any reason to question that Dr. Hackert did *not* have assignment of benefits?"

"No."

"Are you aware that the Court relied upon your testimony in formulating a decision in this matter?"

Muller wasn't going to let it go any further: "That is out of bounds. Next question."

"Well, I'm sorry but —"

"I've already -- you do not speak for the Court, Dr. Hackert."

"Well, I'm not speaking for the Court. I'd like to actually not speak for the Court but *quote* the Court, if I may."

"No. You are asking questions of this witness, and the Court is not

121

a witness."

"Okay. Very good...do *you* believe that Dr. Hackert had assignment of benefits, or do you believe that Dr. Hackert did *not* have assignment of benefits?"

Mr. Leavitt objected: "Lacks foundation and irrelevant what her belief is."

"Sustained. Well, sustained as to foundation. So next question."

With my inquest derailed by the court, Mr. Leavitt elected to re-direct: "I have some clarifying questions."

"All right. And it shifts back for rebuttal testimony, so I'm allowing rebuttal testimony within the scope established by Dr. Hackert's questioning," Mueller explained.

Mr. Leavitt asked Ms. Baron if she was "relying on Dr. Hackert's submission of claims where he marked on Box 13 that he had received assignment of benefits as the basis for your statement in your affidavit," to which she answered in the affirmative.

She was then excused for the day.

Chapter 30

Next was the opportunity for the defense to present its case, and I called myself as a witness.

As a self-represented party the court allowed me a "headline format" of testimony over the usual strict Q&A. My first effort was to bring into evidence one of my exhibits labeled "UUU," which was the existing docket in its entirety. "All right, your Honor. Turning to Exhibit UUU at large, I would like to ask the witness if he recognizes it as a public document, which he does."

"You're talking about the entire Exhibit[]?"

When I confirmed, Judge Mueller blocked: "[W]e're going to talk about UUU outside the presence of the jury first."

At least I tried.

"[A]re there other topics you wish to testify to not involving UUU?"

I again attempted to introduce supportive decisions like *Klay*. "[What] I would like to bring into evidence is based on it's an exception to [the] hearsay rule, and it says that if there is factual information from a public record, such as a civil trial, it may be used as evidence."

Judge Mueller wasn't going to let it happen: "Are there facts that you want to testify to…. [¶] … [¶] That you have personal knowledge of"?

One of my other goals was to "tell my story," and so I turned to a narrative. I shared with the jury my perspective at the time of the procedures in question: claims were submitted on behalf of patients; checkboxes were marked according to industry standards; assistant surgeons are much like pathologists or radiologists whose services are medically necessary and for whom assignment would seem to be implied, even if those parties may never interact with a patient.

Mr. Leavitt was then given the opportunity to cross-examine.

"Dr. Hackert, your narrative was interesting to me, but there's some statements you made that I found very, actually somewhat troubling." Counselor Leavitt then attempted to make me agree that I filed the claims fraudulently.

"[M]y testimony," I resisted, "is that I never intended to falsify any information to Cigna or anyone else."

Because he pressed on I had to reply, "Mr. Leavitt, I'm not sure if you are intentionally misphrasing my testimony or if it was in error, but my testimony was that it would be disruptive if I came into a preop area with a clipboard and a pen and said to a patient I realize you don't know who I am...but you can't have this operation unless you sign this form right here and right now. [T]hat['s just not how it's done."

I'm not sure the court reporter took it down quite right but I also attempted to add that at least some of the Cigna plan documents describe how a provider *may* file a claim "on behalf of the patient" but not necessarily with so-called *direct* assignment.

Mr. Leavitt lastly referenced my deposition. "Isn't it true, Dr. Hackert, that you said on three separate occasions during your deposition that you did not have an assignment of benefits, that it would be impossible for you to get assignment of benefits, and you understood that you never had an assignment of benefits?"

Judge Mueller overruled my objections and I answered: "Well, the answer to the question is when a deposition − I think the deposition was, you know, some hundreds of pages long. And when a question was asked over and over again, I mean, you brought it up three different times, if you're, you know, kind of wearing down a witness, so to speak, the answers get a little bit more abbreviated. So it does not appear that I qualified every answer, but the testimony in the deposition is consistent with the testimony I've just provided. But if it's taken out of context, meaning taken out of the global context, it may seem that I've said to the jury that I believe I had assignment, but I said to you at the time of the deposition that I did not have assignment...."

Rules and decorum do not allow a party to cross-examine the *lawyer*, even though I would've liked to ask Mr. Leavitt if he remembered arguing that my earlier averments regarding not having assignment were *un*true.

I had to wonder what the jurors thought of it all as they were dismissed for the day.

After court was adjourned Judge Mueller returned to some "housekeeping" topics including my request to present to the jury Cigna's prior pleadings which argued that I had assignment, as well as and the court's "express rejection" of my declaration that I did not.

All on transcript, Mr. Leavitt commented that the question of assignment status with respect to the Hackert v. Cigna and Cigna v. Hackert phases "are two completely different issues. The Court got it absolutely correct on the motion to remand and the summary judgment motion, because those were claims that would only be valid if there was an assignment of benefits. So we said okay, that's fine, let's assume you had it. [¶ … [¶] I will say at the end of the day, he never had an assignment of benefits."

You'll remember that Cigna's removal, its opposition to the motion to remand, and its motion for summary judgment all pivoted on their assertion at the time that assignment was *present*. I had already raised the following citations to the court if assignment should be found *absent*:

- [A]ny order or other decision, however designated, that adjudicates fewer than all the claims or the rights and liabilities of fewer than all the parties does not end the action as to any of the claims or parties *and may be revised* at any time before the entry of a judgment adjudicating all the claims and all the parties' rights and liabilities. (Fed. R. Civ. P. 54(b). Emphasis added.)
- If at any time before final judgment it appears that the district court lacks subject matter jurisdiction, the case shall be remanded. (28 U.S.C. § 1447(c).)

Based on the present admission from Cigna's counsel that in its own view I never had assignment, did Judge Mueller announce that she would now be rescinding the ruling on the motion for summary judgment and remanding the case? No, her final comments were "We'll see you in the morning at 8:30. And we'll see the jury at 9:00."

Chapter 31

On the way in for the second day hoping to feel better I played a Chris Isaak song I had come across on one of his albums, *Courthouse*:

> People take their places, down at the Courthouse
> People stand in line to see you fall....
> And I don't care what people say
> I will always feel this way
> I don't care how long it takes
> You're not to blame, you're not to blame

Judge Mueller had agreed to "sleep on" the question of admissibility of the docket and the dispositive cases, and opened the session by asking if I had any supporting authority, a homework assignment of sorts.

Regarding the docket entries that incriminated Cigna's positional shift, I again offered the *Bakshinian* case which advises that "a party's statement in a pleading can be used against that party even if the party later explains that the statement was in error." The pertinent response was, "One reason I'm letting the jury try [the assignment] question is, frankly, the record is very confusing on that point."

Indeed, "contradictory" is a word that comes up amidst the definition of "confused."[26] But Judge Mueller tilted right back to Cigna's side: "I've looked at what Cigna has said in the past. It has not taken the position that you had an assignment in the documents you want to cite. Ms. Baron's declaration doesn't say that. The briefing doesn't say that. It's taken the position that you submitted claims *signaling* that you had an assignment. [¶] ... [¶] I think there's a critical distinction between the characterization of Cigna's taking the position that you had an assignment actually and the representation that you submitted claims indicating you had an assignment."

Doublespeak.

Of course if the judge had come to believe that I did not have assignment all along, the appropriate action now would be to rescind & remand, but I knew that wasn't going to happen.

As another basis to bring into evidence both the earlier docket and supportive opinions like *Klay*, I invoked the "residual exception," Fed. R. Evid. 807: "Under the following circumstances, a hearsay statement is not excluded by the rule against hearsay even if the statement is not specifically covered by a hearsay exception in Rule 803 or 804: (1) the statement has equivalent circumstantial guarantees of trustworthiness; (2) it is offered as evidence of a material fact; (3) it is more probative on the point for which it is offered than any other evidence that the proponent can obtain through reasonable efforts; and (4) admitting it will best serve the purposes of these rules and the interests of justice."

"I'm familiar with it," Judge Mueller quipped and then sidestepped.

I made a last effort to salvage the jury instructions themselves despite the previous day's discussion: "With respect to...assignment, your Honor, my only plea, once again, would be in your initial version, you said...assignment may not be in any particular form or something very close to that. And that wording again has been eliminated in the meantime. But you yourself did recognize that the concept of assignment is a contractual model, and, of course, contracts may be express, implied, or otherwise."

"So that's my other question for this morning," she replied, "the most critical question, I think. Would it be error to add that language in a final instruction, the final assignment instruction, that an assignment can be in different forms, including oral and implicit? So do you have authority? I understand your request to add that, and I'm seriously considering it. I haven't found anything that would tell me it's error. Ultimately -- I mean, I, frankly, can't tell you that I've been able to read the fine print on the back of those forms or if there's any other document currently in the record that clarifies the rules Cigna would say are applicable to the assignment. So, first of all, do you have authority –"

"Yes, your Honor."

"-- that specifically applies in these circumstances where there's an ERISA?"

"Yes," I answered, referencing once again both the *Klay* opinion which contrasts "courtesy" assignment from "direct" assignment, and *Misic* requiring only "valid" assignment "under ERISA," with no mention of being in writing.

Judge Mueller turned to Mr. Leavitt for riposte, who said "*I* don't believe you can have an assignment by implication, but I don't have authority that says you cannot...."

"I will make a final decision then," Judge Mueller concluded.

The jury was then brought in, and Mr. Leavitt continued his cross-examination of me where we had left off the prior afternoon.

First he attempted to make me agree that providers like emergency physicians, anesthesiologists, radiologists, and pathologists are employed by hospitals, even though my limited knowledge was otherwise. I presume he was trying to give the jury an explanation of why a pathologist, for example, isn't seen at a patient's bedside with an operative specimen in one hand and a clipboard in the other demanding the patient sign over benefits.

Next, although the court would not allow *me* to present filings from the Hackert v. Cigna phase of the case, Mr. Leavitt was permitted to introduce an item from within my UUU exhibit, the declaration I had made in support of the motion to remand.

"I want you to read paragraph 3 into the record."

I complied: "Paragraph 3. I am not a fiduciary, beneficiary, or assignee of any beneficiary of any Cigna patient vis-à-vis," V-I-S A V-I-S, "ERISA," capital E-R-I-S-A."

"Now, you signed this declaration under penalty of perjury that you were not an assignee of any beneficiary of any Cigna patient under ERISA. What did you mean by that?"

"My perspective, again, at the time [] these procedures were being performed and the bills were being submitted to Cigna, my understanding was that I was submitting the claims on behalf of the patient, of the given patient as a courtesy. That the form is what it is. It's a form that is set by a government standard. We talked about that, a CMS 1500. That the industry standard calls for using that form. There are essentially no exceptions to that. My billing service has a certain protocol. I followed the protocol. I followed what I thought was the industry standard. And the reason I declared this is because when I brought -- ultimately turned to litigation to resolve the disputes at large, my perspective was that they were at the state law level and not under ERISA. And with respect to how, I would say the word would be contemplated, meaning when the scheme of ERISA, if we overlay the

ERISA scheme on top of the facts and my understanding, I was not an assignee with respect to ERISA. I was filing as a courtesy to the patient but not as so-called having direct assignment."

On redirect examination of myself I testified, "[A]t a point in time in this litigation, it was found that I had assignment," to which Judge Mueller rejoined "[Y]ou're not testifying as a legal expert...So the jury shall disregard that statement because that's, I think, an attempt to make a statement of law. And I will clarify the law for the jury."

"I thought, your Honor, that the *jury* could weigh the evidence as presented to make an assessment."

What was one more demerit now?

I wrapped up revisiting my belief I had the *implied* permission of patients to submit claims on their behalf and certainly was not intending to defraud Cigna.

Mr. Leavitt elected to re-cross-examine: "[P]lease list all the facts that you rely on to conclude that you had now an implied assignment."

It's odd reading a transcript because things don't always come out as clearly as you might hope in such a situation, but I basically said that, as a fact, I did perform surgery on the patients in question in the capacity of an assistant surgeon; that this was medically necessary and had value; that there would seem be an implied agreement for such medical providers to receive compensation in exchange for their work. I suggested that "any reasonable patient would believe that the reimbursement is ultimately due to the provider."

Mr. Leavitt then called Cheri Baron back to the stand for rebuttal, or so he thought.

"Ms. Baron, yesterday we heard testimony from Dr. Hackert that he thought some of the disputed claims had never been paid. I want to ask you did I ask you to review all 29 claims at issue in this litigation?

"You did."

"Did you reach a conclusion as to whether Cigna, on behalf of a self-funded plan, paid all 29 claims?"

"I did."

"Was there any claim that was not paid as alluded to by Dr. Hackert?"

"I'm going by memory, but if my memory serves me correctly, all 29 claims are paid, so we've made a payment on all of them."

"Thank you. Nothing further," Mr. Leavitt concluded.

"All right. Dr. Hackert, any questions?," asked Judge Mueller.

"Yes, your Honor."

I had Ms. Baron turn to the spreadsheet Mr. Leavitt introduced as an exhibit during my deposition, now among the trial exhibits.

When I inquired if she recognized it, Ms. Baron replied "I helped create the document...."

I then set out to complete foundation: "And is this the sort of thing that would be a regular practice of your work to create such a document?"

"It is, yes."

"Do you have any reason to question the authenticity of the contents of what you see in front of you?"

"I have no reason to question it, no."

"Is that type of record kept, is it maintained by you or your organization? Is it something that is maintained as a record?"

"I'd say yes, we do."

"And is it your belief that it was made, that it was created at or near the time of these disputes in question?"

"Maybe because of the dispute."

"You would agree, then, it was made at or near the time of the disputes and by someone with knowledge, namely, you. You have the knowledge because you created it; correct?"

"Yeah. I would say a team of us looked at this and created this."

"All right. And there is no reason to question -- the term would be your competency as a witness. You are capable of providing testimony regarding this; correct?"

"I certainly try my best."

I moved to admit the document into evidence under the "business records exception" characterized in Fed. R. Evid. 803(6), but met resistance from both Mr. Leavitt who objected on relevance and the court itself. That meant the jury wouldn't be allowed to actually *see* the document during this examination, or later during deliberations, but at least Judge Mueller let me continue the line of questioning itself.

"I'd like to look at a certain column within the spreadsheet," and counted with the witness from left to right to a heading titled "Amount Paid By The Plan."

Ms. Baron was given time to look over the multipage spreadsheet, and then asked to tabulate the number of claims where she herself had previously documented no payment had actually been made.

"I'm counting five," she answered.

"Thank you," I said. "No further questions, your Honor."

Mr. Leavitt attempted on redirect to pose a statement-as-question: "That's not the same spreadsheet that's being litigated here today; isn't that true?"

Ms. Baron answered, "That's what I understand."

"*Today* we're seeking claims that were *over*paid to Dr. Hackert or —"

Judge Mueller interrupted Mr. Leavitt's verbal sleight of hand: "At this point we're just talking about an assignment, so I think maybe it was fair impeachment."

What a monumental process to counter a lawyer's efforts to bury the truth.

The jury was temporarily dismissed as Judge Mueller reviewed the *final* jury instructions with the parties, having decided, after all, to reintroduce "implication" as a mode by which assignment may be established. Too late now.

Chapter 32

Closing statements, at last. About time to get this farce over with.

The jury was reseated and Mr. Leavitt went first as counsel to the counterclaimant. He led off by discussing Exhibit 1, the series of claims:

> Box 13 says this: "Insured's or authorized person's signature." All capitalized. Then it says "I authorize payment of medical benefits to the undersigned physician for the services described below." And typed into the form, on every form that Dr. Hackert submitted, in capital letters are these three words: Signature on file. So only one way you could have a signature on file. That is where somebody signs a document, a written document.
>
> Dr. Hackert has reported to Cigna on behalf of Intel and a whole lot of other large employers that he had a written document signature on file saying he could submit this claim to Cigna to be paid by the...employer. [¶] ... [¶] All of these processes exist for one real important reason. And that's to help control what is going on across the country and which we hear on a daily basis is healthcare fraud, healthcare misrepresentation. These protections about having a signature on file are intended to weed out the healthcare fraud that is running rampant through our system, through our country. Medicare, Medicaid. We hear about it daily. Large companies, small companies, large medical groups, single doctors, billing for services that they're not entitled to be paid.

As Mr. Leavitt continued to portray the medical profession as collective frauds, Judge Muller finally said "I think this goes beyond the evidence."

But Mr. Leavitt persisted: "I found [Dr. Hackert's testimony] to be really interesting because this morning, he said the reason he lied on the form and checked that he had the assignment of benefits was because it was more convenient for the passed out patient."

Lawyers are the most skilled ventriloquists of all. Did the jury buy in, or was it likewise repelled? An attorney acquaintance once told me that "the 'L' word" is never to be said in court—"Liar."

Winding down, Mr. Leavitt posed an analogy: "[If] you bring your car to a mechanic and the mechanic needs to have an assistant mechanic[, d]o you get a bill from the head mechanic and the assistant mechanic? No. The mechanic who requests the presence of the assistant mechanic pays the assistant mechanic. The assistant mechanic doesn't separately bill you."

After he finished and yielded the podium for my summation, I presented a contrasting analogy, arguing that assistant surgeon billing *is* unique. "Imagine a presidential election," I asked the jury. The taxpayer is faced with choosing a president, kind of like selecting a primary surgeon. Think of the taxpayer as a patient, and the president as a primary surgeon. Now, the president having been elected has an obligation. He or she is asked to find the best, most qualified vice president to take that post because it's an important role. It's not a copilot really. It's a different job. It has a lot of responsibility. In that model, an *assistant* surgeon would be like a *vice* president. Despite being designated by the president, ought a vice president turn to the *president* for a salary? Is the vice president *employed* by the president? No. It's the treasury that would write a paycheck. But the vice president would need to submit a "time card" of sorts to the *accounting* office, in medical billing, the CMS 1500 form that's submitted to a plan administrator. But, even though this standardized governmental form might appear to require *written* certification from the taxpayer, the vice president would think, "Well, when I submit a request for a paycheck from the treasury via the accounting office, surely the taxpayers have *implied* their willingness to reimburse the work I'm doing for the country, even if they hadn't actually *signed off on* the "time card."

I then compared pathologists and radiologists to a "cabinet," providers who similarly don't turn to "the president" for payment, even if they haven't received *direct* assignment to bill "the treasury" on a patient's behalf.

I left the jury picturing that supposed public benefactors like Cigna and its attorneys were, in reality, *limiting* access to healthcare: "[W]hen these claims were being submitted, I had no idea that this was going to be the result. Obviously if it was, there would have been some alternatives, including saying to the primary surgeons when it comes to a Cigna member, I cannot provide services to that patient unless you can make arrangements with Cigna[,] or the patient can make an arrangement, because I certainly wouldn't want to appear like I am actually somehow committing fraud."

Mr. Leavitt had a few of his originally allotted minutes left, which he used to walk through the jury instructions, concluding with "All you heard is that Dr. Hackert did it as a courtesy, but he never informed any of the patients that he was being courteous."

No good courtesy can remain unpunished?

Chapter 33

Word was received that the jury had reached its unanimous decision. Court was brought back into session, and the deputy read the verdict into the record. "Based on the instruction, the jury finds as to the threshold assignment question: Dr. Hackert was not an assignee."

Judge Mueller thanked the panel and asked them to retire for the present: "[W]e'll let you know I think within the next 15 minutes or so what the schedule will be for the afternoon if we need to continue to call on your services."

With the jury dismissed she turned to the parties: "All right. So as we talked about before the jury returned the verdict, I think this means we now try the misrepresentation claims to the jury. Do the parties agree? Mr. Leavitt?"

From the initial reply of Cigna's counsel one would've had the impression that counterclaimant was putting the tank into drive and swinging about the turret, but Mr. Leavitt then remarked, "I'll be the first to say I think based on Dr. Hackert's testimony, we're going to have a difficult time with fraud...."

During an exchange between judge and counselor about proceeding, among the other causes of action, "with both negligent and fraudulent," Judge Mueller asked Mr. Leavitt "if there was a concession there where you feel as if negligent is sufficient and that's all you want to try. It's up to you."

"Let me have 30 seconds with my client," Mr. Leavitt replied.

"I'll give you a moment to meet and confer...."

During this informal pause I took the opportunity to address the bench regarding the role for a jury on Money Had and Received which I feared the court would still allow Cigna as a blunt tool. "Your Honor...if I could, from the trial brief I submitted, I did point out how the U.S. Supreme Court has identified Money Had and Received as being a *legal* question and therefore triable by a jury and not an *equitable* question[,] and provided other caselaw from California supporting [that]." Judge Mueller invited me to "repeat that once you meet and confer."

A recess was called and the court reporter stepped away from the stenograph.

Chapter 34

Although settlement *discussions* are considered privileged, coming back into open session the court transcript recorded that the parties had arrived at a resolution: "Dr. Hackert and Cigna have reached a settlement," Mr. Leavitt announced to the bench.

Judge Mueller asked the parties to step forward. "So are you prepared now to identify the bullet points?"

"I think we are," said Mr. Leavitt.

"Why don't you say what you think the bullet points are, and we'll see if Dr. Hackert agrees."

"The terms of the settlement," Mr. Leavitt relayed, "are such that Cigna will dismiss its counterclaim and waive all fees and costs. Dr. Hackert will dismiss his claim, his plaintiff's claim, and agrees not to pursue appeal to the Ninth Circuit or any other reviewing court. Essentially the parties are mutually walking away from this dispute, and there is no further litigation of any kind to continue. Dr. Hackert will be responsible for his fees and costs. Cigna will be responsible for its fees and costs. There will be no exchange of money. It is a true mutual walkaway putting an end to this litigation and allowing the parties to move on. Just for final, there will also be no claims of malicious prosecution based on either side's bringing of the original, their original claims."

As requested by Judge Mueller I confirmed the terms Mr. Leavitt had just read into the record, after which she said "Then at this point we'll let the jury know that we no longer need their services.... I'll call them in then so you can also say thank you. Do you want me to tell them there's been a settlement of remaining claims or just say we no longer need their services?"

By sharing this whole story I obviously don't consider justice to have been well served here, but that in no way means I had a personal animus against the judges or adverse counsel. To the contrary, on the first day I made this comment to Judge Mueller amid my motion to dismiss for partiality: "I want to say you're doing an outstanding job technically. I really mean that. But there's a bias that I don't understand the reason for." Even though I don't believe Judge Mueller properly followed the law, she demonstrated a great command of the courtroom. As for Mr. Leavitt, although I pity the *work* he does, I actually liked him on the personal level and don't think I could have offered a better reply to Judge Mueller's question regarding what to tell the jurors: "You know what I would say?...," he proposed, "[a]nd I don't know if Dr. Hackert feels this way. I would like to let them know that their hard work allowed the parties to reach an agreeable settlement." When Judge Mueller turned for my assent I concurred and mentioned once again what an outstanding jury it seemed to be.

Sensing our genuine gratitude, Judge Mueller commented "It is very common in my court, every single time we have a jury, I never fail to be amazed about how serious they take their work, how attentive they are, and how they really do their job as citizen members of the court for the time they're here. So I'm glad that you now have personally experienced that."

The jury was brought back in for a brief word of thanks from the both bench and the parties, then excused.

Following some final administrative remarks Judge Mueller delivered a "Take care" benediction, bringing the trial to its end.

Afterword

A peer to Judge Mueller within the US District Court, Eastern District of California had compiled the following opinion regarding ethics at bar in the case *Moser v. Bret Harte Union High School Dist.*, 366 F. Supp. 2d 944 (E.D. Cal. 2005):

> Federal Rule of Civil Procedure 11...gives the court authority to issue sanctions against a party whose attorney of record signs a 'pleading, written motion, or other paper' [that] is not well grounded in fact.... "The Ninth Circuit has stated: [¶] Under the provisions of Rule 11, when an attorney signs a pleading, he is certifying that he...has read it and that to the best of his...knowledge, information and belief, formed after a reasonable inquiry, it is well grounded in fact.... [¶] ... [¶] Under ABA Model Rules of Professional Conduct, '[a] lawyer shall not knowingly: []make a false statement of fact...to a tribunal or fail to correct a false statement of material fact...previously made to a tribunal...or...offer evidence that the lawyer knows to be false.' American Bar Association Model Rules of Professional Conduct, Rule 3.3.... [¶] ...[¶] Under California law, an attorney may only use methods 'as are consistent with truth....'" Cal. Bus. & Prof.Code § 6068(d).

Is all of that window dressing? Consider the comment by Mr. Leavitt during the trial: "I will say at the end of the day, he never had [] assignment of benefits." Contrast that to Mr. Leavitt's pleadings in opposition to my motion to remand: "The Magistrate Judge was correct in finding that Hackert submitted claims to Cigna as an assignee;" "Plaintiff's claim that he did not receive any assignments of benefits appears to be untrue;" "Plaintiff <u>must</u> be proceeding as an assignee." Were Mr. Leavitt's methods, together, "consistent with truth"? I guess the lawyer joke he shared with me on the day of my deposition mirrors reality: "Don't ever let the facts get in the way of a good case!"

What does the future hold? At the time I segued into surgical assisting the decision seemed quite plausible. My presumption that it would *simplify* professional life proved dead wrong, of course. The battles against unfair reimbursement practices have not been limited to Connecticut General Life Insurance Company, better known as Cigna. What I was correct about, though, is the *need* for qualified assistants. In 2009, Time magazine published an article titled *The Case of the Missing Assistant Surgeon* in which author Dr. Scott Haig made these observations:

> You probably haven't heard much about the assistant surgeon, but all the same, it might interest you to know that we're running out of them. [¶] The combination of hard work, high risk and low pay has made the general surgery specialty nearly as unattractive to new doctors as primary-care medicine. [¶] Many programs have resorted to hiring physician assistants (PAs) [who] can be a truly great help, but they don't have the mind-set of a doctor who stands...in the lead position. When there's trouble, that mind-set is invaluable. And in surgery, sometimes there is trouble. [¶] Most of the surgery in the country takes place in hospitals without residency programs. In these hospitals, the attending surgeon is paid by an insurance company to do the operation (in contrast, at most teaching hospitals, surgeons are either on a fixed salary or part of a group that pools and divides fees) — and he must arrange for another surgeon's help. This used to be easy...when the standard assistant surgeon's payment of 20% of the primary surgeon's fee was a great incentive. Since then...[t]he assistant's share has dropped to 16%, and, more frustratingly, even after spending their time helping they often are not paid at all, with insurance companies saying the services of an assistant surgeon are "unnecessary." [¶] ... [¶] Common sense and unfortunate anecdotes tell us it is unquestionably less safe for the person on the table to have only one doctor

present. But, not surprisingly, no surgeon, hospital, insurance company or government agency has wanted to come up with a hard statistic on how much less safe it actually is. It is clearly against all of their interests to show that assistants are needed.

In the theoretical, supply and demand will at some point intersect, which economists call market "equilibrium."[27] For surgical assisting, however, the lines no longer cross: the supply of assistants has long diverged into a terminal dive, despite the upward trend of the demand curve into the rarefied.

In the past it would've been unusual for me not be in the OR nearly every day of the workweek, but amidst the Cigna case among other negative pressures, I had largely moved on to other projects, working with just a few surgeons who've been willing to accommodate *assistant* assignment into their already extensive patient paperwork.

Sadly, I not infrequently receive requests from surgery schedulers saying they are in "desperate" need of an assistant, but have to explain that I've since dropped privileges at the particular facility or terminated-for-cause former contracts because of unfair payment practices.

One of the insurance companies' most cunning tactics has been to create an environment that pits providers against their own patients and one another. It has generally backfired when I've asked patients to involve themselves with an insurance denial by forwarding on a bill with that advice. One of the surgeons I've worked with voiced his concern and displeasure: "The patient called their primary care physician to complain about being billed by you, who then called me to say they wouldn't be sending me any more patients."

Have we not learned? "Authority always wins."

In the meantime, well after this litigation had come to a close, I received a letter from "Cigna Healthcare" notifying me that "Cigna is terminating its contract with you...because you have not provided us with a completed recredentialing application and/or the information necessary to verify that your credentials continue to meet network participation criteria." Guess they hadn't conferred with Deedee.

Let me leave you with this satirical joke: "We expect to see certain figures out on the golf course...like lawyers, of course...and maybe the clergy.....and also physicians—cutting the grass!" I'm not actually moonlighting as a greenskeeper and find landscaping to be a most honorable and peaceful profession, but hopefully you can find humor in this illustration, and life itself.

Endnotes

[1] Internal quotes and citations often omitted for readability

[2] See https://www.ama-assn.org/amaone/cpt-current-procedural-terminology

[3] See "MultiPlan: Serving Healthcare Payers" at https://www.multiplan.com

[4] https://www.commerce.senate.gov/public/_cache/files/3498904d-6994-4e7d-a353-159261240d54/8C8EF2374162F770AFB94BD373E6B3D9.62409underpaymentstoconsumersbythehealthinsuranceindustryreport.pdf

[5] https://www.dmhc.ca.gov/AbouttheDMHC/LawsRegulations.aspx

[6] Such intermediaries "contract[] with an HMO to provide services for the plan's enrollees, for which it receives compensation on a capitated or fixed payment basis." (*Centinela Freeman Emergency Medical Associates v. Health Net of California, Inc.*, 223 Cal. App. 4th 1366, 168 Cal. Rptr. 3d 91 (Ct. App. 2014).)

[7] Originally at:
http://www.dmhc.ca.gov/FileaComplaint/ProviderComplaintAgainstaPlan/SubmitaProviderComplaint
Archive available at:
https://web.archive.org/web/20150316004651/http://www.dmhc.ca.gov/FileaComplaint/ProviderComplaintAgainstaPlan/SubmitaProviderComplaint.aspx

[8] See, e.g., https://www.dol.gov/general/topic/health-plans/erisa

[9] https://www.cigna.com/about-us

[10] https://profiles.superlawyers.com/california-northern/sacramento/lawyer/curtis-s-leavitt/73016cd5-0bee-4d1b-b504-7c851a170282.html

[11] http://uscode.house.gov

[12] "Fed. R. Civ. P." is an abbreviation for the Federal Rules of Civil Procedure, available at:
https://www.uscourts.gov/rules-policies/current-rules-practice-procedure/federal-rules-civil-procedure

[13] https://www.cms.gov/Medicare/CMS-Forms/CMS-Forms/Downloads/CMS1500.pdf

[14] http://www.caed.uscourts.gov/caednew/index.cfm/judges/all-judges/5055/united-states-magistrate-judge-carolyn-k-delaney-ckd/

[15] Duncan, R. (2010). Win Your Lawsuit: Sue in California Superior Court Without a Lawyer. Berkeley: Nolo.

[16] "In re" is a Latin phrase used in case captions for "In the matter of"

[17] Paraphrased from https://www.hbook.com/1999/01/vhe/our-roots-v/called-horn-book/

[18] Per Black's Law Dictionary, "Ex Rel." is shorthand for the Latin phrase *ex relatione* meaning "by or on the relation of" and describes a suit typically brought by the government upon the application of the private party (called a *relator*) who is interested in the matter.

[19] Rule 3.3(a)(2), Candor Toward the Tribunal, available at:

https://www.americanbar.org/groups/professional_responsibility/publications/model_rules_of_professional_conduct/rule_3_3_candor_toward_the_tribunal/

[20] The narrow common law exception where facts may be re-examined is the "granting of a new trial...for some error of law" per the cross-referenced case, *Parsons v. Bedford*, 28 U.S. 3 Pet. 433, 447, 7 L.Ed. 732 (1830)

[21] Specifically, 29 CFR § 2560.503-1(m)(4)(i) and (f)(2)(iii)(B)

[22] Cigna's "Amended Points and Authorities in Support of Motion for Summary Judgment"

[23] https://www.merriam-webster.com/dictionary/fiat

[24] Latin for "or not"

[25] Latin for "by one's own accord"

[26] https://www.merriam-webster.com/dictionary/confused

[27] https://www.khanacademy.org/economics-finance-domain/microeconomics/supply-demand-equilibrium/market-equilibrium-tutorial/a/market-equilibrium